You are about to secure a timeless overview of Richard Baxter's life ... book was life changing when I rea... will on the one hand thrill the re... a faithful pastoral ministry yet simultaneous... and opportunities. Read it and use it with an eager anticipatio... the pastoral ministry will be transformed.

Harry L. Reeder, III
Pastor, Briarwood Presbyterian Church, Birmingham, Alabama

Richard Baxter's *The Reformed Pastor* is a book that will never go out of print. It is very useful .... This book is a story of a young minister going to a working town (not an Oxford or Cambridge) and by his awakening ministry and pastoral visitation from house to house the whole of that community was pervasively affected, multitudes were given an understanding of the truth of the Christian gospel and a love for the Son of God. The theology and resulting methodology that achieved this in Kidderminster was recorded in this book by Baxter. It became the most accessible and widely read of his many literary productions. It is powerful. Most ministers studying it will feel that they have never begun to be preachers of local congregations, and such a conviction might be the book's greatest blessing today. We are far too satisfied with scraps of praise from our supporters while the churches decline and the world moves on its broad road to destruction. Some of Baxter's writings reflects the chronological gap that separates us from his time, so this valiant and sensitive attempt to make it even more accessible by upgrading the language, giving it a contemporary flavouring, is most welcome.

Geoff Thomas
Minister, Alfred Place Baptist Church, Aberystwyth, Wales

Only the Lord knows the number of pastors who have found inspiration in Richard Baxter's *The Reformed Pastor*, to maintain a vigilant watch over their doctrine, life, and ministry. Full of practical advice and wisdom, well-worn copies have been the companion of faithful Protestant ministers since the 17th century. Sadly, its dated language and historical references have made the work all but inaccessible to many modern pastors. That's why Christian Focus's publication of *The Ministry We Need* is a cause for rejoicing. Prepared by W. Stuart Owen, this abridged and rewritten version presents the burden of Baxter's great work to a new generation. Owen's brief biographical sketch provides an introduction to Baxter's work and the remarkable transformation that took place in Kidderminster under his ministry. Church leaders will find this book a helpful resource for evaluating the personal character of office bearers and for setting a biblical direction for their shepherding care of God's flock.

Charles Wingard
Associate Professor of Practical Theology,
Reformed Theological Seminary, Jackson, Mississippi

A most amazing work that should be read by every young minister before he takes a people under his care. I think the practical part of it should be reviewed every three or four years. Nothing would have a greater tendency to awaken the spirit of a minister to that zeal in his work, for want of which many good men are but shadows of what (by the blessing of God) they might be, if the maxims and measures laid down in that incomparable Treatise were strenuously pursued.

Philip Doddridge (1702–1751)
A well-known Nonconformist pastor in Northampton, England, who ran a small college in his home for training men for the ministry

THE MINISTRY
WE NEED
THE REFORMED PASTOR

Copyright © Grace Publications Trust 2018

paperback ISBN 978-1-5271-0103-6
epub ISBN 978-1-5271-0171-5
mobi ISBN 978-1-5271-0172-2

First Published in 1997 as *The Ministry We Need*
This revised edition published in 2018
in the Christian Heritage Imprint
by
Christian Focus Publications Ltd,
Geanies House, Fearn, Ross-shire,
IV20 1TW, Scotland, U.K.
www.christianfocus.com
and
Grace Publications Trust
7 Arlington Way
London, EC1R 1XA, England.
www.gracepublications.co.uk

Cover design by Pete Barnsley
Printed by Bell & Bain, Glasgow.

MIX
Paper from
responsible sources
FSC® C007785

THE MINISTRY
WE NEED
THE REFORMED PASTOR

RICHARD BAXTER

CHRISTIAN
HERITAGE

Contents

Part 1: The Oversight of Ourselves

Part 2: The Oversight of the Flock

Part 3: The Oversight in Practice

Extract from the Introductory Essay by Dr J. I. Packer

Richard Baxter was the most outstanding pastor and evangelist that Puritanism produced. His achievement at Kidderminster was amazing. England had not before seen a ministry like it. The town contained about two thousand people. They were 'an ignorant, rude and revelling people' when Baxter arrived, but this changed dramatically. 'It pleased God that the converts were so many ... families and considerable numbers at once ... came in'. A century later, when George Whitefield visited Kidderminster, he wrote to a friend: 'I was greatly refreshed to find what a sweet savour of good Mr Baxter's doctrine, works and discipline remained to this day'.

Baxter believed that teaching was the minister's main task. He also believed that Christians should regularly come to their pastor with their problems and ministers should regularly catechise[1] their congregations. Baxter's main concern was that personal catechising should be given to everyone, not just the young. It was this concern that brought *The Reformed Pastor* to birth.

---

1. The verb 'catechise' comes from the Greek 'katecheo' which means 'to teach orally, inform, instruct' (Vine). This method of teaching, by question and answer, was used by the Jews (Acts 18:25; Rom.2:18). The early church adopted this method for teaching young believers the basic truths of Christianity in preparation for baptism. A number of catechisms were prepared at the time of the Reformation including those by Luther and Calvin. The well-known Westminster Shorter Catechism was produced shortly before *The Reformed Pastor* was written. Baxter used the Anglican Prayer Book Catechism which had been finalised in 1604. Like many other catechisms, it was based on The Apostles' Creed, The Ten Commandments, The Lord's Prayer and the nature of the two sacraments.

The ministers of the Worcestershire Association had committed themselves to systematic parochial catechising, on Baxter's plan. They fixed a day of fasting and prayer, to seek God's blessing, and asked Baxter to preach. However, Baxter was too ill to go; so the material he had prepared, *The Reformed Pastor,* was published. By 'Reformed' he means, not Calvinistic in doctrine, but renewed in practice. 'If God would but reform the ministry,' Baxter wrote, 'and set them on their duties zealously and faithfully, the people would certainly be reformed. All churches either rise or fall as the ministry doth rise or fall.'

The Reformed Pastor was, and is, dynamite, and it made its mark at once. 'The Lord hath revealed his secret things to you', wrote Thomas Wadsworth to Baxter, 'for which many a thousand souls in England, shall rise up and bless God for you'. An anonymous letter says: 'Mr Baxter's *Reformed Pastor* was extraordinary ... I am obliged to bless God and thank Mr Baxter and wish with all my heart all young ministers ... would diligently and frequently peruse it.' Baxter wrote about 1665, 'It prevailed with many ministers to set upon that work which I there exhort them to. Even from beyond the seas, I have had letters of request, to direct them...'.

Baxter died, but his book lived on. John Wesley's father Samuel wrote: 'I wish I had the *Reformed Pastor* again which I lost when my house was last burnt ... He (Baxter) had a strange pathos and fire.' John himself told the Methodist Conference: 'Every travelling preacher must instruct them from house to house... Can we find a better method of doing this than Baxter's? His whole tract... is well worth a capable perusal'. Charles Wesley and William Grimshaw of Haworth agreed that preachers should 'visit from house to house, after Mr Baxter's manner'. In 1810, Francis Asbury, the Methodist apostle of America, wrote: 'O what a prize: Baxter's *Reformed Pastor* fell into my hands this morning'. John Angell James wrote, 'I have made, next to the Bible, Baxter's *Reformed Pastor* my rule as regards the object of my ministry'. Spurgeon frequently used to have his wife read it to him on Sunday evenings.

Has Baxter's book a ministry to ministers today? Three qualities which mark it justify the answer 'yes'.

The first is its energy. Sylvester says that Baxter wrote as he spoke, and his words were passionate, for they came from the heart as well as the head. His book blazes with white-hot zeal, evangelistic fervour and eagerness to convince. What comes from Baxter's passionate heart has energy and power, and can still go to the heart across a three-centuries gap.

Then, second, the book has reality. Any Christian who loves his neighbour and who seriously believes those without Christ are lost will make evangelism his main task in life. Otherwise he undermines the credibility of his faith. If he cannot take his faith seriously, why should anyone else? Nowhere is this inconsistency more forcefully exposed than in *The Reformed Pastor*. Who will question our need of such reality today, and in the ministry most of all?

Third, the book is a model of rationality. Baxter knew that men are dead in sin, and only God can convert them. However, he also knew that God uses means, and that grace enters by the understanding. So Baxter insisted that ministers must preach as men who feel what they say. They must also deal with individuals, because preaching alone often fails to bring things home to ordinary people. So it was in Baxter's day. Is it not so now?

The Reformed Pastor faces the modern minister with at least these questions. (1) Do I believe the gospel Baxter believed?

(2) Do I then share Baxter's view of the vital necessity of conversion? (3) Am I then as real as I should be in letting this shape my life and work? (4) Am I as rational as I should be in choosing means to the end I desire, and am charged to seek? Have I sought to find the best way of regularly talking to my people personally about their spiritual lives? How to do this today would have to be worked out in terms of present circumstances, which are very different from those Baxter knew. However, Baxter's question to us is, should we not be attempting to practise this constantly? If he convinces us that we should, it will not be beyond us to find a suitable method of doing it. Where there's a will, there's a way! Now we had better leave Baxter to speak for himself.

Extract from the Preface by William Brown[1]

Of the excellence of this work, it is scarcely possible to speak in too high terms. It is not a complete directory of pastoral theology, and in this respect it may, by some, be considered as defective; but, for powerful, pathetic (appealing), pungent (stirring), heart-piercing address, we know of no work on the pastoral office to be compared with it. Could we suppose it to be read by an angel, or by some other being possessed of an unfallen nature, the reasonings and expostulations of our author would be felt to be altogether irresistible; and hard must be the heart of that minister, who can read it without being moved, melted and overwhelmed, under a sense of his own shortcomings; hard must be his heart, if he be not moved to greater faithfulness, diligence and activity in winning souls to Christ. It is a work worthy of being printed in letters of gold: it deserves, at least, to be engraven on the heart of every minister.

But, with all its excellencies, the *'Reformed Pastor'*, as originally published by our author, labours under considerable defects, especially as regards its usefulness in the present day. We may often, with advantage, throw out extraneous matter from the writings of Baxter; but there are few men's works which less admit of abridgement. This sacrifices their fullness and richness of illustration, enervates their energy, and evaporates their power and pathos. While, however, I have made these changes from the original, I trust I have not injured, but on the contrary, improved the work.

1. A nineteenth-century Scots minister who wrote the first abridgement on which this version is based.

Before I conclude, I cannot help suggesting to the friends of religion that they could not perhaps do more good at less expense than by presenting copies of this work to the ministers of Christ throughout the country. There is no class of the community on whom the prosperity of the church of Christ so much depends as on its ministers. If their zeal and activity languish, the interests of religion are likely to languish in proportion; while, on the other hand, whatever is calculated to stimulate their zeal and activity is likely to promote, in a proportional degree, the interests of religion. They are the chief instruments through whom good is to be effected in any country. How important, then, must it be to stir them up to holy zeal and activity in the cause of the Redeemer! A tract given to a poor man may be the means of his conversion; but a work such as this, presented to a minister, may, through his increased faithfulness and energy, prove the conversion of multitudes. Ministers themselves are not perhaps sufficiently disposed to purchase works of this kind: they are more ready to purchase books which will assist them than such as will stimulate them in their work. If, therefore, any plan could be devised for presenting a copy of it to every minister of the various denominations throughout the United Kingdom, what incalculable good might be effected! There are many individuals to whom it would be no great burden to purchase twenty, fifty or a hundred copies of such a work as this, and to send it to ministers in different parts of the country; or several individuals might unite together for this purpose. I can scarcely conceive any way in which they would be likely to be more useful. To the different Missionary Societies, I trust I may be allowed to make a similar suggestion. To furnish every missionary, or at least every Missionary Station, with a copy of the *Reformed Pastor* would, I doubt not, be a powerful means of promoting the grand object of Christian missions. Sure I am of this, there is no work so much calculated to stimulate a missionary to holy zeal and activity in his evangelistic labours.

Edinburgh
12 March 1829

Dedication by Richard Baxter

To my beloved brethren, the faithful ministers of Jesus Christ:

The subject of this book is very relevant to you and to your churches. This encourages me to write, even though I am unworthy to be your teacher. Firstly, I should explain why I wrote this book and my style of writing.

Some time ago, the Lord showed some of His servants their need to catechise[1] everyone in their parishes. Before starting, they wanted to humble themselves before God because of their previous neglect and to seek His help. A meeting was arranged for this purpose at Worcester on 4 December 1655. I was among those asked to preach, and so I prepared this message. It is rather long, but I only intended to preach those parts I considered most relevant at the time! Illness prevented my preaching, so my brethren asked me to publish this material instead.

Some may think I am too outspoken, especially at a time when others are attacking the ministry.[2] That is true, but I have not changed my mind for these reasons:

1. We could not be humbled without confessing our sins.
2. It was our own sins we were confessing so no one else should be offended.
3. I had no time to translate it into Latin so that only the learned could read it.

---

1. See footnote 1 p. 9.
2. Roman Catholics and some extremist Protestant groups were all attacking the ministry for various reasons at this time.

4. When sin is so obvious, it is both useless and even more sinful to try and hide it.

5. A free confession is necessary for a full pardon, and when sin is public the confession should also be public.

6. So many in the ministry are self-seeking, negligent, proud, etc. that it has become our duty to admonish them. It would be cruel to leave them alone as long as there is some hope. The best way to reform the church is to reform her leaders. Souls are perishing while they pursue their worldly interests and pleasures, or quarrel with their brethren! We cannot be quiet while men are going to hell and the church is being ruined. That is why, at the risk of appearing offensive, we should admonish the guilty even if they do not like it.

My first and main point is that it is the duty of ministers to catechise those committed to their care. These are my reasons:

1. We all agree that people should be taught the truths of Christianity, especially the way of salvation.

2. I trust we all agree they should be taught in the most helpful and effective way.

3. It is undeniable that personal questioning and teaching has many advantages.

4. Personal instruction was used by Christ, the apostles and by godly ministers in every age.

5. We should surely care for all people, not just our congregations.

6. This work evidently deserves much of our time.

I therefore urge you, for our Saviour's sake, to give yourself wholeheartedly to this work. I have found it a most effective way of bringing the gospel to people. It also reinforces the preaching ministry.

At first I was uncertain about the work. I thought people would be uncooperative or I would not have the time or energy. However, I found the obstacles were much less than expected, and were far outweighed by the benefits. Few are uncooperative and make excuses. Those who come make more progress in personal godliness than from all our public preaching.

This kind of work is sanctioned by the Scriptures, previous church practice and your consciences! The Westminster Directory[3] says, 'It is the duty of the minister not only to teach the people ... in public, but privately, and particularly to admonish, exhort, reprove and comfort them, etc...'. Is there anyone who has the least spark of grace and love for God who could oppose or refuse to do this work? If there is they should be ashamed of themselves. How can you pray for the salvation of sinners and then neglect one of the most effective ways of spreading the gospel? I hope every godly and able-bodied minister in England will now begin this work. Those who are opposed because of unworthy motives will have to answer for the blood of souls before the judgment seat of Christ.

My second request is that every minister would practise church discipline. The usual excuse is that people will not stand for it. But surely, the truth is that you cannot be bothered. If we neglect discipline the result will be disorder and the loss of godly members to more disciplined churches.

---

3. A handbook for church practice and worship produced by the Westminster Assembly.

My final request is that all faithful ministers of Christ would be united and regularly meet together for mutual encouragement and instruction.

Please excuse the faults in this book. I earnestly pray for the success of your labours against all the powers of darkness.

Your unworthy fellow servant
Richard Baxter
15 April 1656

Introductory Note

Pay careful attention to yourselves and to all the flock, in which the Holy Spirit has made you overseers, to care for the church of God, which he obtained with his own blood.

Acts 20:28

Some believe this passage implies that Paul had authority over the Ephesian elders. However, we are not claiming any superiority. If we ministers are called to teach our own people, then we may also teach each other. We struggle with the same sins and we live by the same faith as they do. Yet we have greater tasks and greater difficulties. We therefore need at least as much ministry. Our text clearly shows that Paul shared this belief. Every minister would greatly benefit themselves and the entire church if they seriously considered these verses!

I propose to speak on this text as follows:

First, to consider what it means to look after ourselves.
Secondly, to show why we need to look after ourselves.
Thirdly, to inquire what it means to look after all the flock.
Fourthly, to show the way in which we should look after all the flock.
Fifthly, to state some motives why we should look after all the flock.
Lastly, to make some application of the whole.

Part 1. The Oversight of Ourselves

Section 1. The Nature of this Oversight

1. Firstly, look after yourselves. Make sure you are truly converted yourself. Take care that while preaching Christ to others, you are not without Christ yourself. A glorious reward is promised to faithful preachers of the gospel, but you will never enjoy that reward unless you receive the gospel yourself. There are many preachers now in hell who once warned their hearers many times to escape it. Do you expect God to save you for offering salvation to others if you reject it yourself? God never promised to save preachers, no matter how gifted they are, unless they are converted.

To be unsaved is awful, but to be an unsaved preacher is much worse. Are you not afraid to open your Bible to read your own condemnation? When you preach the gospel are you not increasing your guilt by rejecting the Saviour you proclaim? Yet an unsaved preacher is usually unaware of his condition. He daily handles precious truths. He lives an outwardly holy life. He denounces sin in others and urges them to be holy. How tragic: to starve with the bread of life in your hands, urging others to eat. If this is true of you then take my advice, preach to yourself before preaching any more to others. Will it help you in the day of judgment to say, 'Lord, Lord, we have prophesied in your name', only to hear the awful words, 'Depart from me, I do not know you'. I advise you to confess your sin before your people and ask them to pray for their minister's conversion!

It is not unusual to find ministers who are unconverted. Your preaching will be cold and lifeless if Christ is not in your heart. O that every theology student understood this. What is the point of study if it does not lead to a knowledge of God and His saving grace? If God graciously saves them they will then have such a knowledge of Him they never dreamed of before. Nothing can be rightly known unless God is known. Nothing in the entire universe can be properly known until it is known in relation to the Creator.

When God made man he was perfect and lived in a perfect world. Everything revealed the glory of God. If man had not sinned, he would have increased in the knowledge of God and of himself. But, when he sought knowledge for himself, he lost the true knowledge of God and His creation. Instead, the knowledge he gained was vain and empty.

Christ's work is to restore us, by faith, to the purity, obedience and love in which man was first created. Therefore, the most holy men are the best students of God's creation. The study of science is worthless if God is not sought in it. To see and adore, to love and delight in God as revealed in His creation is the only true wisdom. It is therefore a danger in education to place other subjects before the study of God. Theology should come first and guide us in all our studies. Nature should be read as one of God's books which He made to reveal Himself. The books of Job and Psalms teach us that science and theology are not so unrelated as some think.

I therefore urge all Christian teachers to tell their pupils about God and His salvation alongside the sciences. Do not think they are too young to understand the Word of God. You have little idea what lasting impressions your words might make. You are in a uniquely privileged position of having young people willing to listen. When religion is treated like any other subject, godliness is stifled! How few students are serious and godly! What greater service could you do than if you could be the means, under God, of their conversion?

2. Be diligent to keep yourselves in a spiritually fit and healthy condition. Preach your sermons to yourself first. Your people will notice if you have spent much time with God and they will benefit. What is most in your hearts is likely to be most in their ears. I confess that when my heart is cold, my preaching is cold. If our love or faith or reverence declines it soon shows in our preaching, maybe not in what we preach but in the way we preach it, and our people will suffer. However, if we are filled with love, faith and zeal then our ministry will bring spiritual refreshment and encouragement.

Brethren, watch your hearts. Keep them free from lusts and passions and worldliness. Maintain your faith, love and zeal. Spend much time with God. If you do not then everything will be wrong. You must fetch from Him the heavenly fire to consume your sacrifices. If your fervour is artificial you cannot expect God's blessing. Shameful sins and heresies usually start in a small way. Satan often appears as an angel of light to draw you back into darkness. If you yield to pride or fall into error you will become a curse instead of a blessing to God's people. Therefore watch, for your own sakes as well as for others.

I think a minister should be especially careful of his heart before public ministry. Read some spiritually stimulating book, or consider the great importance of your message, or think of your people's great spiritual needs. Go in the zeal of the Lord so that those who come along cold may have their hearts warmed before they leave.

3. Make sure your lifestyle agrees with your teaching. If it does not you will undo all the good you have done. If our lives are inconsistent people will think there is little truth in Christianity and our preaching is just 'hot air'! If we mean what we say then we will surely do what we say. One proud word, one flash of temper, one selfish action can soon destroy all your labours. If you do not long for the success of the gospel what are you doing in the ministry? Are you not prepared to endure insult or injury, to control your temper, to curb your pride, or befriend the lowly to win souls? How strange that some preach so carefully yet live so carelessly. We should take great care that we do what the word says and are not speakers only, deceiving ourselves (see James 1:22). We should be as careful about the way we live as the way we preach. If we want to win souls then this will be our aim whether we are in the pulpit or out of it! Be diligent to use everything that you have for God, as well as your tongue!

Maintain a manner of conduct and speech that is beyond reproach. Your lives should condemn sin and inspire godliness in every way. If you want your people to care well for their families then care well for your own. There is nothing like meekness and self-denial for overcoming prejudice. Resist the temptation to use your authority to pressurise people into respect and submission. Be a friend to everyone, especially the poorest members. This can be an efficient way of doing much good!

I urge you to be generous and compassionate. Use your material resources to meet the needs of others. Buy spiritually edifying books for your people. He is no true Christian who has anything he is not ready to give away, if Christ asks for it. If more ministers practised self-denial it would open more hearts to receive their message than all their preaching.

Religion without self-denial is hypocrisy. We do not need to live in a monastery, but we should use all we have for Christ.

4. Make sure that you do not fall into those sins you condemn in others. How can you exalt Christ as Lord if you break His laws? It is easier to condemn sin than to overcome it. Take care that you keep under your bodies, and bring them into subjection: so that after you have preached to others, you yourself will not be disqualified for the prize (see 1 Cor. 9:27).

5. Make sure you have what it takes to be a good minister of Jesus Christ. There are many difficulties to resolve, even in the basics of Christianity. We have duties that are too difficult for many to do. We have to warn our people about many subtle temptations so they can escape them. We have much prejudice and obstinacy to overcome. Great skill is needed to make the truth plain to everyone's conscience! Much ability is required to answer all the devious arguments against the truth. Great wisdom is needed in counselling. Is all this something anyone can do? Do you not think you need to make every effort to equip yourself for such demanding work? Skimping your studies will not help you to be a good preacher. God alone can equip us and help us. But if we are lazy and neglect the means He has given we will quench the Holy Spirit. Therefore, waste no time! Study and pray, investigate and practise! That is the way to improve our skills.

Section 2. Motives for Watching over Ourselves

1. Look after yourselves because, like others, you have a heaven to win or lose. You may preach the gospel and even lead others to Christ, but without holiness you can never be saved. You can preach about Christ and yet neglect Him, about the Spirit and resist Him, about faith and yet remain unbelieving, about conversion and stay unconverted, about heaven while remaining worldly. You may be the greatest preacher in the world, but without grace in your heart you will remain unsaved. Preachers of the gospel will be judged by the gospel. Therefore, take care because you have a soul that will be saved or lost eternally.

2. Like everyone else you have a fallen nature with sinful tendencies. If sinless Adam fell because he failed to keep watch, how much more should we take care! Just as one small spark can start a forest fire one sin often leads to another. Even the holiest saints have the remains of pride, unbelief, self-ambition and every other sin. We are easily enticed by foolishness or lust and then judgment is distorted, zeal is cooled and diligence is slackened. If you are not careful your treacherous heart will soon find an opportunity to deceive you. Sins you thought were uprooted long ago will revive. Because you are so weak and prone to sin you must carefully watch yourself.

3. Take care because you are Satan's special target. As Christ's servant you are a serious threat to Satan's powers. He knows that if you fall your people will be easy prey. Against you he will use his most subtle suggestions, persistent enticements and fiercest attacks. Satan can disguise himself as an angel of light. He can easily outwit the most intelligent of men without them realising it. You may think you have advanced in your faith when in fact you have betrayed Christ. You will not even see the hook or line, much less the subtle angler, while he is tempting you with his bait. This bait will be so adapted to your nature and temperament that you will definitely be attracted by it. If Satan succeeds in ruining you he will then use you to ruin others. What a triumph for Satan if he can make you unfaithful or tempt you to sin. He will reproach the church and say, 'This is your godly preacher'. He will glory against Christ and say, 'I can turn your best servants into traitors.' Finally, he will accuse you as one who has disgraced his calling. Therefore, watch yourself carefully and do not give Satan the opportunity to gloat over your downfall.

4. Look after yourselves because you are being carefully watched by many. If you fail in any way everyone will hear about it. Others may sin unnoticed, but you cannot. You should be thankful because this will help you to be careful. Therefore live as someone whose life is exposed to the full gaze of the public eye. There are spiteful people who would be delighted to pounce on your least mistake. If they cannot find any faults they may even invent them. Therefore, how carefully should we live before so many evil-minded observers.

5. Look after yourselves because your sins involve more guilt.
   a)   Since you know more than others you are more likely to sin against the light.
   b)   Your sins involve more hypocrisy. Your task is to preach against sin, exposing its vile nature. Can you then privately indulge it? Will you be the enemy of sin in public but its friend in secret?
   c)   Your sins are more treacherous. Every Christian declares their allegiance with Christ against sin. As a minister that allegiance is greater. Every time you preach about sin or judgment and every time you administer baptism or the Lord's Supper it implies your denial of sin and union with Christ. What a traitor you are if you then allow sin the least place in your heart!

6. Look after yourselves because your duties require special grace. Lesser gifts and abilities may be sufficient for less-demanding duties. However, if you become a minister of the gospel you will need more than ordinary grace. You should be really sure that God has called you and equipped you for this work. Some who served Christ well in a less-exacting role have entered the ministry only to bring disaster on the church. If you want to fight the Lord's battles and bear the burdens of the ministry you will certainly need to look after yourself.

7. Look after yourselves because the Lord's honour depends on it. The closer we are to God the more our failures bring dishonour on His name. God's honour, for a true Christian, is more precious than life itself. Could you bear to hear people throw the filth of your sins in the face of God? Think of the heartbreak your fellow Christians would suffer because of your

offences. Therefore, be careful of every word you speak and every move you make because God's reputation in the world is your responsibility. If you fail, God will restore His own honour but your own disgrace will not be so easily removed.

8. Look after yourselves because the success of your work depends on it. God seldom uses men who are unfit for the great work of the gospel.

    a)   Can you expect God to use men who live for themselves and not for His glory? Some enter the ministry as a career or to gain respect or a reputation for themselves or for other selfish reasons. Is it surprising when God does not bless such a ministry? The results of their work are only what you would expect from natural causes.

    b)   Can you expect to be successful if you are unfaithful or half-hearted in your work? If your faith is only intellectual and your fervour just emotion, your preaching will be useless. Can you seriously call sinners to repent if you have never appreciated the vileness of sin or the value of holiness? Can you pity others, pointing them to Christ if you have no pity on yourself to do the same? It is impossible to love others more than yourself. You cannot warn people about hell if you do not believe it exists. If you want to be a soul winner you should firmly believe the Word of God and in the life to come, and live a life of holiness and zeal. Whoever neglects their own soul is unfit to care for others.

    c)   Is it possible to fight against Satan if you are his servant? That is what an unconverted person is. That is why many ministers of religion are enemies of

Christ. They may talk about Christ and godliness, but secretly they do all they can against Him. They slander those who love and obey Christ as fanatics or hypocrites. The most dangerous enemy is the enemy within. They may seem to be sound preachers, but inwardly they are gripped by worldliness, pride, unbelief and an aversion to godliness. Hypocrites can seem sincere because it is easier to speak against sin than to overcome it. They may be happy for others to repent while they continue to enjoy their secret lusts. You cannot earnestly fight against sin and Satan unless you hate them as destroyers of men's souls and as enemies of Christ. Far from hating sin, an unbeliever loves it most of all. Such a man is totally unfit to lead God's people or to plead with others to renounce the world and the flesh.

d) People will not take that man seriously whose life does not match his preaching. They will think he does not mean what he says if he does not do what he says. If someone says the house is on fire while relaxing in an armchair you will think they are joking. People are more ready to believe what they see rather than what they hear. They will think your preaching against sin is empty talk if they see you are selfish or worldly or careless. It would be like telling them, 'This is the way to live. There is no harm or danger'. If you fail to correct sinful talking or behaviour or to tell people their need of Christ, they will think these are unimportant. Furthermore, this will give them an excuse to criticise more godly men saying, 'They upset us with talk of judgment and hell while you laugh and joke with us'. They will think you only preach because you are paid to do it. Is that man fit to be a minister of Christ who speaks for him on Sunday while the rest of the week he lives to please himself?

Finally, remember that the success of your labours depends entirely on the Lord's blessing. Christ has promised His faithful servants His presence with them, His Holy Spirit in them, His word on their lips and Satan's defeat before them. There are no such promises for unfaithful servants. In fact unfaithfulness will cause Him to leave you and bring all your efforts to ruin. In His sovereignty God may possibly use you to do some good to His people, but that would be unusual. To some extent this also applies to godly servants if they are backslidden.

Part 2. The Oversight of the Flock

Section 1. The Nature of this Oversight

We should firstly notice some things assumed by our text (Acts 20:28).

It assumes that every local church will have its own pastor and every pastor His own church. The Lord's people should recognise those he has provided to care for them. A pastor without a church should minister wherever he has opportunity. Otherwise his first responsibility is to care for his own people and minister elsewhere only in his spare time or in times of special need.

It also assumes that there will not be more people in our churches than we can possibly look after. God does not ask us to do the impossible. He will not give us responsibility for so many that we are unable to know and care for each one in the way He requires. Caring for souls requires authority to exercise discipline as well as ability to teach. A pastor may occasionally have to look after more people than he can properly care for, but that is neither usual nor desirable. He can then only do what he can which is less than a pastor would normally do.

Let us now consider what it means to 'keep watch over all the flock'. Notice it is 'all the flock' or every individual member of our congregations. That means we must know each one: their character, their interests, their weaknesses, their besetting sins, etc.... Then we should look after them. Like Christ, the Good Shepherd, who left the ninety-nine to seek the one who was lost, so we should watch over every individual. There are many examples in Scripture of prophets and apostles who were sent to minister to individuals.

You may say your congregation is too large for you to do this. But, did you not know that before you were called to the church? If you did, why were you unconcerned about being faithful to your calling? Have you honestly made every effort to obtain an assistant? Are you willing to make some sacrifices so the church can support a fellow worker? That would surely be better than allowing the care of the fellowship to be neglected. You may say your family could not live on less, but are there not many families in your church who live on less? Some in the past were happy to preach the gospel for less and today some are even prepared to preach for nothing! Is it not better to beg for bread than to put the salvation of souls at risk?

While we can only be saved by the grace of God, yet no one can be saved without knowing the truth. People are more likely to know the truth if they are instructed personally. If I have an assistant this could be done, and if I live more simply I can have an assistant. Does not all that we have and are belong to God? Is not one soul more valuable than the whole world? Is it not inhuman to allow souls to perish because we want a higher standard of living? If we expect our people to practise self-denial should we not deny ourselves? Should we not deny ourselves more than others since our salaries come from offerings devoted to the gospel of Christ? Should we not therefore use our money for that purpose as much as possible? While we are called to look after all the flock, some need our special care.

1. We should especially aim at the conversion of unbelievers. This should be our main objective for which we work with all our might. The plight of unbelievers is so great they deserve our greatest sympathy. If a believer sins they will be forgiven. God will not allow them to continue in sin and He will finally make them perfect. However, unbelievers are '[without] hope and without God in the world' (Eph. 2:12). Surely we would rush to help a dying person rather than someone who is only slightly injured. Can we be unmoved by the needs of those heading for judgment and eternal condemnation? I can almost see them entering hell at this moment! I can almost hear their desperate cries for help! Their plight is particularly tragic because they have no desire to ask for help themselves. Often I cannot find it in my heart to stop pleading with sinners to satisfy the curiosity of those who want to hear something different. Have we the same spirit as Christ who was moved to weep over the impenitent? How little do we value souls if we keep quiet while sinners go to hell! Would we even allow our worst enemy to suffer like that and not make the least effort to help? Whatever else you may neglect, make sure you do not fail to plead, persuade and urge sinners to turn to Christ for salvation.

2. We should always be ready to counsel those seeking spiritual advice. A pastor should be able to care for his people's spiritual health as much as a doctor looks after our physical health. A pastor should be able to resolve the doubts and difficulties of those who come to him. It is a pity that most ministers keep quiet about this aspect of their work. We should not only make people aware, but positively encourage them to come to us for spiritual advice. Therefore, make sure you are well prepared to give good counsel on a whole range of

spiritual issues, especially those concerning the great matter of salvation. One good word of advice may be more helpful than many sermons.

3. We should aim to build up believers in their faith. This should be done in a variety of ways according to the various states of Christians.

    a)   Many have been Christians for a long time but seem content with little growth. They are reluctant to make the effort to serve the Lord or to grow in grace. Weak believers have little discernment and are easily led astray. They find it difficult to benefit from the ministry or to delight in God and His ways. They little realise how immature they are and they easily succumb to temptation. They are of little use to God or to their fellow believers. Their condition is so serious we should work hard to nurture their faith. Christians who are strong in faith and love bring honour to Christ. Unbelievers are more receptive to the gospel when they can see lives wonderfully changed by it. Therefore, it is very important to strengthen the faith of weak believers and to equip them for Christian service.

    b)   Some Christians need special help because of some particular sin that is preventing their growth in grace. It is our duty to help them overcome their pride or worldly ambition or hasty temper or whatever. We should show them its evil nature and give them directions for dealing with it. We should not be lenient with sin either in believers or unbelievers. Some may resent our admonition. However, if we are to be faithful to Christ we must deal firmly and lovingly with our straying brother.

c) Another group needing our special attention are backsliders. It is tragic to see believers going back to ungodly ways and bringing dishonour on the Lord's name. We should work hard to try and restore them. Backsliding is a gradual process that finally ends in apostasy unless the Lord prevents it. We are to 'restore … in a spirit of gentleness' those who are caught in a sin (Gal. 6:1). Only make sure their restoration is thorough. They should give clear evidence their repentance is genuine and should fully confess their sin. Great wisdom is needed in dealing with such cases.

d) Finally, we need to look after those who are strong in the faith. They need our help to maintain their spiritual vitality. They also need help to make further progress and to be equipped for greater service for the Lord.

4. We should especially care for families. The peace and prosperity of both church and society depend greatly on good family relationships. The influence of godly parents can greatly help the ministry. In contrast, worldly and prayerless parents are liable to dampen their children's interest in Christianity. Therefore, if you want the work of the gospel to flourish, I urge you to do all you can to promote godliness in the home. This may be done in several ways:

a) Get to know each family so you will then know how best to help them.

b) Visit them occasionally when everyone is at home. Ask the parents whether they pray or read the Bible with their children. Try convincing them that neglecting this responsibility is sinful. If you have time show them how to do it. It is a good idea to get them to promise to be more conscientious in future.

c) Difficulty in prayer is usually caused by neglect. The sinfulness of this should be explained to them. Even beggars know how to ask for help. For a start they could use written prayers. However, this should only be something temporary because true prayer comes from the heart and will vary according to the needs and circumstances at the time.

d) Make sure every family has some good Christian books apart from the Bible. Encourage them to read these books in their spare time and especially on Sundays.

e) Encourage them to keep Sunday special by avoiding worldly interests and pleasures. Encourage parents to discuss the Bible lessons with their children. Unless family religion is promoted it is unlikely you will see the gospel flourish in your community either now or in the future.

5. We should be diligent in visiting the sick. Throughout our lives we should be growing in godliness and preparing ourselves for eternity. However, this need is felt more acutely in times of illness. Who can be unmoved by the eternal needs of someone whose life is ending? To think their soul will soon be in heaven or in hell should stir our deepest compassion. The most stubborn sinners will usually listen to us on their deathbed. The most hardened unbelievers are ready to change when they see death approaching. I agree this is not true repentance in most cases. However, even though few are saved

on their deathbeds, we should do all we can to point them to Christ. This is not intended to be a manual of pastoral work, but I would suggest some ways in which we can help those approaching death.

a)   Do not wait until they have deteriorated to the point where they are unable to benefit from your ministry. Visit them as soon as you hear of their illness whether invited or not.

b)   Since time may be short, concentrate on those truths most likely to bring them to peace with God. Tell them about the joys of heaven, of the One who died to bring us there, of their foolishness in neglecting Him so long. Yet they may still receive the gift of eternal life if they repent of their sins and trust in Christ alone.

c)   If they recover, remind them of the promises they made when they were ill. This has been the means of bringing many to Christ and so it is important to keep reminding them of their need to be right with God.

6. The final part of our work to consider is church discipline.

a)   We should confront those who profess to be Christians but whose lives are inconsistent. We should firstly see them in private before bringing them before the church leadership. The way we deal with them should be appropriate for each individual. However, we should speak clearly and firmly to shake them out of their apathy. We should help them to see what damage their sin is doing both to themselves and to the gospel.

b) If they remain defiant we should bring them before the church and again urge them to repent. This is in obedience to Christ's command (Matt.18:17). This was always practised in the early church until corruption and formality crept in. Many ministers would be ashamed to neglect preaching or praying, but think little of neglecting church discipline. Some say that public reproof does little good. I reply:

- What right do we have to question the duties God has clearly given us?
- Church discipline is essential to expose sin and to maintain the purity of the church.
- Church discipline gives the sinner a final opportunity of restoration.
- Discipline acts as a deterrent to keep others from offending.

c) The offender should not only be rebuked but also encouraged to repent and confess their guilt before the church. If they think their sin is insignificant we should use Scripture to show them its true seriousness. Fellowship cannot be restored unless the church is satisfied repentance is genuine. This should be obvious from a change in attitude and behaviour.

d) We need a great deal of godly wisdom to avoid doing more harm than good. We also need great humility, even when we have to be severe. We should avoid giving any impression we are motivated by selfish reasons such as pride or envy. We should make it clear to everyone that we are acting in obedience to God.

e) The church should pray for the offender. This is especially important if they refuse to be present at the church meeting or if they show no signs of regret.

In that case we should encourage our people to pray fervently to the Lord for their restoration.

f) Those who truly repent should be fully restored to the fellowship. We should not trivialise their sin by being too lenient, nor should we discourage them by being too severe. There should be a confession of guilt and a promise to avoid such sins in future. They should learn to avoid temptation and rely not on themselves but on the grace of God. We should then assure them of forgiveness and acceptance with God through the blood of Christ. The fellowship should also forgive them and not remind them of past failures. Finally, we should thank God for their restoration and pray He will keep them in the way of holiness.

g) Those who remain impenitent must be excommunicated. Its purpose is to exclude the offender from the privileges of fellowship until they repent. The people should be advised not to have any fellowship with them. However, everyone should continue to pray for their repentance and restoration.

If pastors were more conscientious and diligent in exercising church discipline this would bring many benefits. Those who are afraid of giving offence or facing difficulties can hardly expect much blessing.

Section 2. The Manner of this Oversight

1. Our whole aim should be the glory of God and the salvation of souls. Selfish motives will corrupt our work no matter how good our deeds may be in themselves. If our motives are not right, even our best sermon is no more than a glorious sin.

2. The work of the ministry is so vitally important that we should give it our utmost energy and diligence. Therefore, study hard because the task is great and our minds are weak. Our aim is no less than to overcome evil and to establish the kingdom of Christ. Can this be achieved by a casual or indifferent approach? If you are negligent souls may be lost and you will be held responsible.

3. The work should be carried out in a sensible and orderly manner. Our teaching should be adapted to the needs and abilities of our hearers. We should begin by thoroughly teaching the fundamentals of repentance and faith in Christ. Young believers need the 'milk of the word', while mature believers need more substantial teaching.

4. Our ministry should concentrate on the great teachings of Scripture. That is what people need to feed their souls, to destroy their sins and to warm their hearts. If we only preach Christ we will preach everything. This is the best way to avoid wasting time. Many other things are desirable, but

time is short and souls are precious. If people fail to grasp the great essentials they will be lost forever. This will not please those who like to hear something new and exciting. We may often repeat ourselves because essential truths are relatively few. However, we should use variety in their presentation. Beware of imitating those who try to compensate for spiritual emptiness with a show of learning or humour.

5. Our teaching should be as plain and simple as possible. People cannot benefit from our ministry unless they understand it. If we obscure the truth we are enemies of the truth. If we cannot teach a subject clearly it usually means we have not understood it clearly. Some ministers keep quiet about certain doctrines because they think people are too prejudiced to accept them. But surely, the best way of overcoming prejudice is to explain the facts and make the issues as clear as possible. Some doctrines are difficult to grasp and we should consider our people's limitations. It is nevertheless our duty to work hard at making all our teaching so clear and simple that even the slowest can understand.

6. We should fulfil our duties with great humility. Remember the word 'minister' means one who serves. Pride is out of place in one who seeks to help others along the lowly way of salvation. If God expelled a proud angel from heaven will He welcome a proud preacher? Pride generates envy and quarrelling and greatly hinders the work of the gospel. Some pastors have become incompetent because they are too proud to learn. We should not arrogantly dismiss anyone who disagrees with us. We should always be ready to learn from others.

7. Our ministry should have a careful balance of authority and gentleness. The exact balance will depend on the type of persons and situations we are dealing with. Without authority people will ignore us while excessive authority will turn them against us.

8. We should be serious, earnest and fervent in all our work. Our task demands more ability and zeal than we can possibly give it. It is no small matter to stand before a congregation and deliver a message from the living God. The seriousness of our calling condemns coldness and dullness. If we want to awaken others we must be thoroughly awakened ourselves. If our words are not sharp they will never pierce stony hearts.

9. Our entire service should be one of sincere love for our people. They should be convinced that we care for their highest interests in all we do. We should love them more tenderly than a mother caring for her child. We should imitate Christ, the Good Shepherd, who laid down His own life for His sheep. If our people are convinced we love them they will be more receptive to our teaching. We should therefore demonstrate our love in practical ways. Only take care your love is Christ-centred not self-centred. They should follow Christ not us. Do not ignore their sins. Reproof is not inconsistent with love. God himself 'disciplines those he loves'. If you want to be their best friends, help them against their worst enemies.

10. We must exercise much patience in our work. We should be prepared for many disappointments. Some of those for whom you have prayed fervently, preached earnestly and helped practically will treat you with ridicule and contempt. We should bear patiently with their unkindness and keep

trying to help them. We must not react with pride or anger. Many ministers fail in this respect.

11. We must have reverence in all our work. Reverence comes from knowing God. Irreverence in holy things is therefore a sign of hypocrisy. One who preaches as though seeing the face of God has a far more profound effect than an irreverent man even though they preach more eloquently and fervently. I detest preaching that is amusing or light-hearted. We were not sent to entertain but to impress sinners with the majesty of our holy God. The more God's presence is apparent in our ministry the more profoundly will it influence people.

12. We must do all things spiritually as men under the Holy Spirit's authority. There is a spiritual note in some men's preaching which spiritual hearers detect and enjoy. Where that is missing even spiritual truths seem ordinary. The proofs and illustrations we use should be spiritual, that is biblical. Scholarship and learning must always submit to Scripture. The most gifted preacher must glory in nothing except the Cross of Christ. It is a sure sign of spiritual decay when we lose our relish for the Word of God.

13. You must earnestly desire and expect results if you want your work to succeed. Unless you long for conversions and spiritual growth you are unlikely to see any. With that hope in mind you should study, pray and preach. God seldom blesses anyone's work unless their heart is set on its success. Can we be content just to receive compliments and salaries? There are times of barrenness in the ministry, but God will then give us grace to persevere. However, that grace is only given to faithful servants and they always long for success. If

I saw no conversions after many years I would think it was an indication God wanted me to work elsewhere.

14. We must keenly feel our insufficiency and complete dependence on Christ. We must continually plead with God for all the necessary grace and energy for our great task. We cannot preach earnestly to our people if we do not pray fervently for them. God alone can give them repentance and faith and eternal life.

15. We should do all we can to promote love and unity between faithful pastors and their churches. We should understand how essential this is for the cause of the gospel and for the good of all believers. We should take every opportunity to promote true spiritual unity. We detest the arrogance of those preachers who denounce others in order to gain a reputation for 'soundness'. Unity should be based on Scripture alone rather than creeds or confessions. Avoid quarrelling over words and try to really understand other people's point of view before dismissing them as apostate. If we are agreed on the great fundamental truths of Scripture we can unite for fellowship. Meetings can be held to deal with misunderstandings, to promote fellowship and to further the work of the gospel. If all the time and energy spent on quarrels had been used to strengthen others in the faith it would have done much good.

Section 3. Motives for Caring for the Flock

1. The first motive comes from our relationship with the flock as overseers of it.

    a) The biblical emphasis is on the work rather than the honour attached to the office (1 Tim. 3:1; Titus 1:7). Many ministers seem to have plenty of time for relaxation and leisure. Have they understood what a demanding work this is? We are called, under Christ, to lead our people in spiritual warfare. It would be enough to have only one willing person to teach, but we have many who are unwilling. We must reason with many who have little ability to reason. They spend little time with us compared with all the time they are in the world. Their worries, cares and pleasures can easily stifle the word you have preached. Their unbelieving hearts can readily extinguish the light of truth. Some who seemed converted turn back to ungodly ways or succumb to pride or error. If we are negligent, even true believers will decline in grace. We should not be discouraged by these difficulties, but we must always be faithful and diligent.

    b) Remember you volunteered for this work. Therefore, even common honesty requires you to be faithful.

    c) Just think what an honour it is to be ambassadors of Christ, calling sinners to be reconciled to Him. How petty of ministers to squabble over positions of honour. They have great ambitions for privilege but little desire for work! If they expended their energy on preaching the gospel instead they would have eternal honour and glory. If they learned to serve Christ with faithfulness, humility and self-denial they would do well.

d) Remember that along with your privileges go great responsibilities. You are fully supported by others so that you may give yourself fully to the work. While others are employed in ordinary work you have the privilege of studying God's Word. Your greatest joy and privilege is studying Christ and proclaiming Him to others. These happy privileges should constrain us to do our work wholeheartedly.

e) Your work unites you to Christ as well as to your people. Christ always takes good care of His faithful servants. He has often rescued them from persecution and strife. Have you considered why the Lord so wonderfully preserves you? It is so that you might fulfil the task He has given you to do.

2. Our second motive is that it is the Holy Spirit who has made us overseers. He has equipped us and led God's people to set us apart for this ministry. The disciples left everything when Christ called them. Our calling is not so direct or extraordinary, but it is of the same Spirit. If God has called us what a great obligation we have to obey!

3. The third motive comes from the greatness of our charge. The church is the body of Christ, the centrepiece of God's plan for the universe. Can we neglect the care of God's children, the fellow heirs of Christ? To be a 'doorkeeper in God's house'

would be a great honour, but we are called to be leaders of God's people! Surely this most glorious calling of all is worthy of our greatest efforts.

4. The final motive comes from the price that was paid: 'the church of God, which he purchased with his own blood'. Shall we despise the blood of Christ by thinking His people are not worth our best care? Shall we neglect souls who were bought at such a great price? If Christ came from glory to seek them will you not go in search of them? If He suffered so much to save them will you not deny yourself for them? As we look upon the gathered people of God, remember they have been bought with the blood of Christ. Listen to that blood[1] pleading with you to be faithful in all your work.

The apostle Paul elsewhere gives many other motives to arouse us to our work. However, these are enough if the Holy Spirit applies them to our consciences.

---

1.   See Hebrews 12:24.

Part 3. The Oversight in practice

Section 1. The Need for Humiliation

We cannot seek God's blessing unless we humble ourselves before Him because of our past failures. We will not be motivated for change unless we grieve in spirit. If we are not humbled how can we expect our people to be humbled? Can we soften their hearts while ours remain hard? Some think their only duty is to preach while it is their people's duty to repent. But, in Scripture, leaders such as Daniel and Ezra sorrowfully confessed their own sins as well as the people's. Can we read Paul's message to the Ephesian elders without feeling deeply humbled? I am sure you all believe that sorrow for sin and confession are necessary to maintain fellowship with God. However, knowing what to do is not enough. Our affections and wills must also play their part. We must confess our sins before God who is 'faithful and just to forgive us and cleanse us'. I include myself since I am aware of so many sins I cannot pretend to be innocent before God.

We only have time to mention the worst sins. However, despite our failings, there are many faithful, gifted pastors in this country, for whom I thank God. I pray the Lord will continue to raise up men for the ministry. That is the best way to promote the work of the gospel and to dispel the error and confusion that abounds in the church today.

1. One of our worst sins is *pride*. Pride afflicts even the best of us. It affects our speech, the company we keep and even our appearance. It fills the mind with ambition and resentment towards any who get in our way. Pride is always insinuating its way into our thoughts and desires. It follows us into our studies. God wants our message to be clear and simple for everyone to understand, but pride prompts us to be witty and clever. Pride blunts the cutting edge of our sermons by excluding anything that seems coarse and unrefined. Pride makes us aim at impressing people rather than edifying them. God wants us to preach fervently, pleading with sinners to repent, but pride tells us to tone it down in case people think we are insane. In this way pride gains control of our ministry. The truth may be preached, but its manner and effect serves Satan's interests more than God's.

After pride has influenced our preparation it then follows us into the pulpit. It affects our preaching style and prevents us saying anything offensive no matter how necessary. Pride makes us please our audience, seeking our own glory rather than the glory of God. It aims to impress people with our eloquence, knowledge, sense of humour, godliness, etc... Afterwards, pride follows us down from the pulpit, making us eager to know what people thought of us. If they were pleased we are overjoyed, but if they were unimpressed we are dismayed. We hardly bother to know whether anyone was saved.

Some ministers are so eager for popularity they envy more famous brethren. They seem to think their God-given gifts are for people to admire. If other men have greater gifts they are overrated! Have we forgotten that Christ gives us gifts to benefit the whole church? If our brother's gifts glorify God and benefit His people should we not thank the Lord? Yet, how often do we find ministers secretly smearing the reputations of more gifted brethren. When they find little to criticise they even stoop to raising suspicions or dropping malicious hints. Others, afraid of losing popularity, refuse better preachers access to their pulpits. This attitude is so common that we rarely find two equally gifted preachers working harmoniously together in the same church. Their friendship is usually cooled by envy and rivalry. Some ministers are so jealous for their position they will try to do everything themselves rather than employ an assistant. This brings the ministry into disrepute and a loss of pastoral care to God's people.

Some ministers think they are always right, even in details, and criticise anyone who disagrees with them. They reject the doctrine of papal infallibility but seem ambitious to be little popes themselves! They expect everyone to agree with them as if they were inerrant. Their excuse is that they are only being zealous for the truth. But, if that is so, why, if proved wrong, do they get so upset as if personally insulted? Some errors become so attached to certain famous preachers that it seems we cannot refute the error without insulting them. They seem to think, if proved wrong on one point, their whole reputation is lost. Therefore they staunchly defend everything they ever said.

We tend to love those who share our opinions and help our cause. We should avoid unkind criticism or hurting others' reputations insofar as integrity allows. However, we resent those who expose our faults especially if it is done in public. Pride makes us think those who disagree with us are biased and quarrelsome. Some are so pompous they only listen to flattery and compliments.

I am horrified that this most evil of sins is so trivialised that people see nothing wrong when it appears in those who are supposed to be godly. When we rebuke unbelievers for sins of the flesh we expect them to be grateful. But if we expose the sins of ministers they react as if they had been outrageously insulted! I am ashamed to admit that pride has become so obvious in our sermons and writings that everyone can see it. We have dishonoured ourselves by idolising our honour. True godliness cannot exist unless pride is hated, mourned over and fought against. However, if symptoms of pride are a sure sign of ungodliness then godly pastors are very rare indeed! There are some, by the grace of God, who are so meek and humble they are examples to the rest of us. They are wellpleasing to God and to everyone, even unbelievers. I wish we were all like them!

O that God would show us how evil pride is so that we might be truly sorry and earnest for change. Pride is Satan's main characteristic. Those who oppose him the most should resemble him the least. Humility in a believer is not an optional extra but an essential quality of the new nature. A proud Christian is a contradiction in terms. Christ teaches us to be 'humble and lowly'. As we see Him washing His disciples' feet should we not feel ashamed of our pride? Are we too proud to associate with poor and needy people who need our help the most? What have we really got to be proud of? Our bodies? They will soon rot in the grave. Are we proud of our humility? That would be absurd. Are we proud of our knowledge? Why, the more you know the more you should realise how ignorant you are! If it is our business to teach others humility, should we not also practise humility? People notice ambitious ministers who love to have pre-eminence and authority over others. In discussions they are not interested in listening to others, only having their own way. Arrogant people are the first to notice pride in others, but the last to see it in themselves.

Let us be honest with ourselves. Can we commend humility to others if we have little ourselves? Can we condemn pride while we indulge it? We tell thieves or adulterers they cannot be saved unless they forsake their sin, and can we be saved if we are not humble? In fact, pride is worse than stealing or adultery. We can appear to be holy and preach faithfully, but we may be as hell-bound as those whose sins are more obvious. Holiness is living for God and sin is living for self. No one lives less for God and more for self than a proud man. You may be a great preacher, but you may preach to feed your ego rather than glorify God. Remember the many ways we are tempted by pride in our ministry. Having a mere reputation for godliness is no substitute for the real thing! How marvellous when people flock to hear us, hang on our words and become our followers. How delightful to enjoy popularity and fame as a great preacher. But then, the temptation to think of ourselves as a great leader of the church becomes almost irresistible.

Therefore, watch yourselves and in all your studies do not forget to study humility. I confess my own need for continual watchfulness. Remember, 'God resists the proud, but gives grace to the humble.' Almost everyone prefers a humble person to a proud one. That is why proud men often pretend to be humble. We need to be very wary of pride because no sin is so ingrained in our nature or more difficult to overcome.

2. Another great failing is that we do not give the Lord's work all the energy and devotion it deserves. I thank God for zealous pastors, but they are sadly rare. I will give some examples to show why we need to confess this sin:

a) We are negligent in our studies. Few take the trouble to be informed enough for the work of the ministry. Some think of study as a tedious chore. We should be eager for the truth, especially about God and His Word. Knowing our ignorance and the greatness of our responsibilities should drive us to search for knowledge. Our work requires us to be well informed about many subjects. Studying for sermon preparation is not enough. Do not merely gather facts, but study how to preach in a way that grips the heart and stirs the conscience. If we are to reason effectively we should not rely on spontaneous ideas. We must be well prepared in advance. Men do not become wise without rigorous study and experience.

b) If we were really dedicated to our work we would give it more energy and enthusiasm. Few preach about heaven or hell as if they really believed in their existence. Sermons are often so tame and boring that sinners take no notice. Some preach with great vehemence, but what they say is often irrelevant. People dismiss it as hot air. On the other hand, it is tragic to hear good teaching wasted for lack of practical application or earnest persuasion.

Remember that people will either spend eternity in a state of happiness or misery. This will make you speak with earnestness and compassion. Never talk glibly about heaven or hell. You will never bring sinners to repentance by telling jokes or interesting stories. Nothing is less suitable for treatment with frivolity or dullness. How can you speak of God or His great salvation in a cold and lifeless way? Remember, unbelievers must be awakened or condemned and a drowsy preacher is unlikely to be the means of awakening them. I am not suggesting you constantly preach at full volume, but you must always be serious. When your subject demands it, preach with all the passion and intensity you can muster. It is the Holy Spirit who draws sinners to Christ. However, He generally uses means, which includes not only what we say but the way we say it. For many, even our pronunciation and tone of speech are important. Preaching that is earnest, powerful and convincing is sadly rare.

Avoid all affectation, but speak as though addressing each person individually. This personal element is sadly lacking in most sermons. Preaching involves a direct contact between souls. Our minds, emotions and wills should all be involved in communicating the truth and love of Christ. Speak as though people's lives depended on it. Satan will not easily submit. We must besiege his strongholds and break down every barrier raised against the gospel. We must reason so clearly from Scripture that sinners must either accept the truth or deliberately reject it. The greatest truths will not move people unless they are movingly delivered. A well-composed sermon that lacks light and vitality is like a well-dressed corpse!

c) If we were truly devoted to the gospel we would show more concern for churches without pastors. Why not help them find a suitable pastor? In the meantime, could we not find time to preach there occasionally? Evangelistic sermons in such places could do much good.

3. Another indication of our lack of commitment to Christ is the worldliness amongst us. I will give just three examples:

    a) The ease with which most ministers can change to suit their worldly interests. For example, between the reigns of Edward VI, Mary and Elizabeth I, thousands of ministers switched allegiance from Protestant to Roman Catholic and back again. Few were prepared to flee the country or suffer martyrdom for conscience's sake[1]. Since pastors differ greatly in personality, background, intelligence, etc. we would also expect some differences in belief. But most of them just 'followed the crowd'. Sadly, this also seems to be true of us today so that our critics can accuse us of being governed by worldly advantage rather than by principle.

    b) Our excessive involvement with the concerns of this life. Some appear to have little desire to be freed from worldly cares to give themselves more fully to the work of the ministry. They seem reluctant to do those duties which could involve financial loss. For example, some are unwilling to exercise church discipline because it could lead to a reduction in the church's income. How can they possibly warn others about the dangers of covetousness? Simon Magus sinned by offering money for the gift of God. How much more sinful is it to betray our ministry for money?

    c) Our lack of generosity and failure to use everything we have for Christ. If ministers were more unselfish they could do more for God. Providing material help for the needy is a very effective way of winning

---

1. We have seen something similar during the last one hundred years in the rapid advance of liberalism in practically every major denomination.

people's trust and making them more inclined to listen to us. If you are unselfish, people will be less suspicious of your motives and more prepared to believe you really care for them. It would be a serious mistake to underestimate how much good this can do. It is one of the best ways of overcoming the prejudice that hinders people seeking Christ. You cannot give what you do not have, but all we do have should be devoted to Christ. The usual excuse is that we must look after our families. To this I answer:

- This is often just an excuse for greedy self-interest.
- We must do our best for our children, but we do not need to leave them a large inheritance. We must strike a fine balance between supporting our families and the church. Those fully committed to Christ, with a loving, self-denying spirit are most qualified to know how to divide their resources.
- Some must marry because of sexual desire, but I believe others could make more effort to control their desires. An unmarried pastor is free from many worries and cares endured by married men. They are therefore able to put more time and effort into the work of the ministry.
- Those pastors who marry should, if possible, choose a partner who is able to support herself and the children. If not, he should support them at an affordable level so he can devote as much as possible to the work of the gospel. I do not want to overburden anyone, but I give this advice knowing how our fallen natures incline

us to indulge ourselves and our families. We are easily deceived into thinking that luxuries are necessities.

If we lived more simply we could do more in the Lord's service. What an abundance of opportunities there is to serve Christ in the world. We can never please everyone, but we should at least strive to 'always keep a clear conscience before God and man'. The more we earn the more we should support the Lord's work. Some well-paid ministers with many people to care for think they only need to preach. If they gave some of their salaries to support an assistant, their people would receive greater benefit. Men may consider us excellent preachers, but beware lest Christ considers us unfaithful. Many have a reputation for heavenly mindedness yet their hearts are too occupied with worldly concerns.

4. We are guilty of undervaluing the peace and unity of the church. Most Christians claim to appreciate the need for love and harmony between believers, but they do little to encourage it. Most promote their own group or denomination as if it alone mattered. The term 'Catholic' is misused by the Church of Rome, but that is no reason to disregard the great truth of the unity of all believers.[2] Some sections of the church are very corrupt, and it would be difficult to have close fellowship with them. Nevertheless, it is our duty to do all we can to help them and to promote unity wherever possible.

How few really take to heart the sufferings of their fellow Christians. How rare to find someone genuinely grieved over the church's sad divisions. Some even seem glad when a rival

---

2. The true Catholic Church is the body to which every true Christian belongs since they have been united with Christ by saving faith in His Person and work of salvation.

church suffers setbacks. They seem to think the prosperity of the entire church is tied up with their own particular group. Few seem to understand the differences between Christians. Those who do understand often use their knowledge to justify their position. If someone is eager to promote Christian unity they are viewed with suspicion. This is because those who deny the essentials of the faith[3] are often calling for greater toleration and liberty.

We have at least as many divisions amongst believers in this country as any nation has ever known. Most of the differences are about forms of church government.[4] If everyone was filled with brotherly love and realised the urgent need for unity, our differences could be overcome. We might not agree on everything, but we could have fellowship based on the great fundamental truths of the gospel. We talk and preach a lot about unity, but, to our shame, we do little. There are those who criticise moves towards evangelical unity. They seem to think the peace of the church is a threat to her purity. But, experience teaches that unity promotes godliness and godliness promotes unity. On the other hand, error breeds strife and strife is bred and fed by error.

It is tragic to see those who should be helping each other in their faith being divisive and contentious. Brotherly love is a hallmark of true faith. The love that confines itself to one's own group is not Christian love. Opponents often receive more envy and bitterness than brotherly love. True believers cannot be dominated by this attitude, but it is so common it makes us question the sincerity of some. There may be

---

3. Baxter was referring to Socinians who denied Christ's virgin birth, His deity, His work of atonement, etc... Their modern counterparts are the modernists or liberals. They are also keen to promote 'unity' based on unscriptural ideas of Christian freedom and toleration.

4   This was the main difference between believers in Baxter's day.

few troublemakers, but they influence many, and this sours relationships between believers. It also makes true religion seem so repulsive to many non-Christians that they continue in their superstition and unbelief. Some contentious ministers are very godly and gifted men. They do not intend to harden sinners in their unbelief, but that is what they are effectively doing. It is not rare to find good intentions in wrong actions. I do not like to say these things. I would prefer not to risk offending those I respect in many ways. But it is Christ I must please and no man's friendship can compensate for the loss of souls. God is my Master, His Word is my rule, His work is my calling and saving souls is my aim. We will never achieve unity until we return to the simple faith and love of the early church. I therefore urge my brethren to unite on the basis of the fundamental truths of Scripture and to bear with one another in other matters. For this purpose I recommend:

a) Do not overemphasise issues over which wise and godly men differ.

b) Do not overemphasise controversial issues that are matters of speculation.

c) Avoid controversies due to misunderstandings about the use of words.

d) Do not overemphasise obscure doctrines that were unheard of by former generations of believers.

e) Avoid adopting beliefs that were either not held or opposed by wise and godly men in any previous age of the church.

I am aware of those who say they believe Scripture and the creeds and yet follow Socinianism[5] or other heresies. But they may also slip through any other test of faith you may think

---

5. See footnote 3 p. 65.

of. Also, your new creed will probably create more divisions unless you adhere very closely to Scripture. It will be a happy day when church leaders are as zealous to heal our divisions as they now are to create them. I believe the moderation I am advocating will then be appreciated by everyone.

5. Finally, I believe we neglect essential duties too much, especially church discipline. When duties demand effort and self-sacrifice how many excuses do we find! In many churches discipline is minimal. Church discipline is discussed much but practised little! Many ministers hardly know their people, never admonish the disobedient or excommunicate the obstinate. They think it is enough to withhold the Lord's Supper. They never call the rebellious to repentance and open confession. Brethren, let us stop making excuses. Do you want your people to realise the value of church discipline? Then demonstrate it by practising it. If we fail to discipline offenders we are allowing the ungodly to rule the church. This will bring us into conflict with God Himself. Many churches are so disorderly it is not surprising that godly members leave for more disciplined fellowships.

Every Christian believes that baptism and the Lord's Supper are essential. And is discipline not essential? Would your people be satisfied if you gave them a glimpse of the bread and wine and never let them take these symbols of their Redeemer's love? Will they be satisfied to hear about church government and never see it in operation? Weakness here will undermine the credibility of your whole position. If you do not practise church discipline it is as good as saying you do not believe in it. I do not want you to rush recklessly into this duty, but when do you intend to start? Would you wait for the right season to start preaching or administering the Lord's

Supper? I know some face more difficulties than others, but that can never excuse neglecting our duty. Seriously consider the following:

a) What a poor example we set before our people if we fail to do our duty!

b) We betray our laziness and maybe even unfaithfulness if we neglect discipline. I speak from experience. It was idleness that kept me from tackling this issue for so long. It is difficult, demanding and infuriates the ungodly. But, since when is an easy life or friendship with unbelievers more important than the approval of Christ?

c) If we fail to admonish the ungodly they will think we are condoning their sin.

d) If we fail to maintain the separateness and purity of the fellowship, people will think there is no difference between the church and the world.

e) We will encourage schism. If we tolerate sin, conscientious believers will think it is their duty to separate from us.

f) We will turn God against us. Christ warned the church in Pergamos because they tolerated heresy and immorality. If we also tolerate sin we can expect the same.

What prevents us from exercising biblical church discipline? Is it the difficulty of the work and the opposition we are likely to encounter? Are you afraid your work would be undermined and your position threatened? Do you think it is impossible to admonish every offender? I reply:

a) These arguments could be used against the practice of every Christian duty. Christ warned us about the world's hatred if we are true to Him. If you are not prepared to suffer for Christ, why did you enter His service in the first place? You can only avoid persecution by unfaithfulness to Christ.

b) You will encounter hostility whenever and however you oppose sin. But, you can always trust God to bless His means of ensuring the health of His church. If you admonish sinners and excommunicate the impenitent you may be helping others to be more watchful. It may also help bring the impenitent to their senses. Above all, God is honoured and His people are distinguished from the world when sin is not tolerated among them.

c) The difficulties are less than we imagine and are out-weighed by great benefits. I believe that ministers who neglect discipline should be dismissed.

That is all I want to say about our sins at this time. All we have to do now is to confess our guilt and humble ourselves before God. Can we honestly claim we have served the Lord in the way He expects? Will we now harden our hearts and conceal our failures? All the criticisms aimed at us may be signs of God's anger. God's judgments on our nation may be partly our fault. If judgment begins at the house of God, then surely, repentance must begin there also.

Can we excuse our sins while calling others to confession and repentance? Is it not better to glorify God in humble confession than to try concealing our guilt to protect our reputations? Would that not increase our guilt and bring further judgments upon us? Surely, it is the sin that is shameful not the confession. Confession is the only way to recovery. I am sure that every true servant of Christ will now respond by admitting their sins before their people and promising change.

69

Section 2. Motives for the Work

Now that we have admitted our guilt it is clear what we have to do. I therefore urge you to start catechising every willing person in your church or area.

Article 1

Firstly, some reasons to motivate you in this ministry.

The benefits of catechising

I rejoice to think of the benefits this work could bring to the church if it is blessed by God and well managed by ourselves. It is a work that should cause everyone to rejoice, even generations to come. Thousands or even millions of people could eventually receive blessing from it. That thought should turn this day of mourning into one of great joy. I thank God He has awakened so many pastors to see the need. Catechising is not a controversial or a new idea. It is just a more intensive and effective way of caring for souls. Surely, every true pastor wants to be a more effective servant of Christ. Therefore, I will list some of the benefits to increase your eagerness for the work.

1. We believe it will bring sinners to the Saviour because it combines two essential elements of evangelism. Firstly, the understanding must be enlightened, and, secondly, the heart

must be changed by the power of the truth. Catechising is a very effective means of promoting both:

a)   In its content: it makes clear the most basic and vital teachings of Scripture.

b)   In its method: by teaching people individually we may have the opportunity to apply the truth to their hearts and consciences.

If people learn the catechism they are more likely to understand the truth. People can often understand ordinary conversation when they have difficulty following a sermon. As we interview them we can find how much they do understand, and then help them with their difficulties or questions. This gives us a good opportunity for pressing home God's Word in a personal way. It also helps apply the truth to their situation. We can also encourage people to use the means of grace to change their lifestyle.

If this can be a means of delivering many souls from darkness then it is well worth all our efforts. It should be a great incentive to think of those you could have the joy of presenting faultless before Christ in glory. Every true minister of Christ longs for the gathering in of God's elect. Remember that when you are speaking to an unbeliever you may be the means of bringing them to Christ. Angels will then rejoice, Christ Himself will rejoice, Satan will be cast out and God's family increased.

2. This work will strengthen the faith of believers. There is a definite order in teaching the truth. You cannot build on a faulty foundation. People must be established in the fundamentals before they can make progress. The basic teachings must vitally affect their whole lives, strengthening obedience

and resistance to temptation. Therefore it is well worthwhile recommending every believer to learn a catechism.

3. It will help people to derive more benefit from our preaching. Those who are well grounded in basic doctrine can follow our arguments and understand what we are saying more easily.

4. Personal counselling helps cultivate good relationships with our people. This makes them more receptive to our ministry. If we keep ourselves aloof we are more likely to be misunderstood. This could be a real hindrance to our ministry.

5. It is an excellent way of discovering each person's spiritual state. We will then know how best to preach to them and pray for them. It also enables us to help them with their difficulties and overcoming their besetting sins.

6. It will help us identify those who are fit to receive the Lord's Supper. We could examine them especially for this purpose, but that is more likely to cause resentment. It is also much better than a hasty inquiry just before the Communion service.

7. It is a good way of showing people what the ministry is all about. They think caring for souls is little more than preaching, administering the sacraments and visiting the sick. It is regrettable that some well-known ministers confine their evangelistic efforts to preaching. This often has little effect because they neglect personal evangelism. This is so common that most ministers no longer consider personal work a part of their duty. However, I am confident that if some of us began this work it would, by the grace of God, awaken many others to their responsibility. What would you think of a doctor

who only treated his patients with a lecture on medicine? A pastor needs to deal with people personally and individually as much as a doctor.

8. It will help people to understand their duty towards their pastors. People do not realise they have a duty to come to us for help with spiritual problems, doubts and temptations. When we visit they sometimes think we are interfering or domineering. They question our right to admonish them. They little understand that the Lord has given us this authority for their benefit. If we rescued them from drowning or pulled them from a burning house would they question the right we had to save them? Some people regard private catechising and instruction as something new and strange. But, if we all persevered in this duty, it would be increasingly seen as something normal, beneficial and acceptable. It would be wonderful if everyone came to regard their minister as a personal counsellor as well as a preacher. Diligence in our work is the best way to change people's attitudes.

9. It will give our political leaders a better understanding of the pastoral ministry. This may help win their sympathy and support for our cause.[1] The scarcity of good ministers is a

1. In Baxter's day, Parliament passed several acts which were designed to promote the cause of the gospel. Amongst them were measures to provide ministers for spiritually needy areas of the country. For example, as a result of an act passed in 1649, one hundred and fifty ministers were settled in the thirteen counties of Wales. Baxter's argument is therefore not strictly applicable to our own situation today. However, it remains our duty not only to pray for our political leaders, but also to encourage them to pursue good and just policies and that the work and witness of the church will not be hindered or restricted. In that sense, therefore, there is a continuing need to demonstrate the value of biblical Christianity as a great benefit to society at large. There also remains the need for planting churches in spiritually needy areas. However, that is not a government matter but the responsibility of God's people.

hindrance to the work of the gospel. There are multitudes of sinners in our large towns and cities urgently needing spiritual help. Many are ready to listen if we take time to speak personally with them. But we do not have the time to speak to so many. We stick to preaching because we can reach more people that way.

We were already overstretched before we began catechising. We now set apart two days a week for the work. To achieve this we had to sacrifice time spent in sermon preparation. Our preaching may suffer, but we cannot neglect teaching individuals. We believe the work will bear fruit. However, if we could do more we feel sure more would be achieved. Some ministers have more people than they can possibly care for. I cannot understand why the authorities do not allow for more ministers in such places. They might be persuaded to do more if they could see good results from our work. However, if pastors are lazy and negligent the authorities will see little point in promoting such a ministry.

10. It will greatly help the future work of the ministry. People are creatures of habit. We have to overcome a lot of resistance if we are to change established customs. Now is as good a time as ever to reform the church. If we delay, it will make things harder for the next generation. The more progress we make the easier it will be for those who follow us. How wonderful if, by God's grace, our labours today lead to great advances for the gospel in days to come.

11. It will promote family religion and a better use of Sundays. We can encourage parents to teach their children a catechism and portions of Scripture on Sundays. This would be a good

use of time previously wasted. By teaching their children the parents may also teach themselves.

12. It will help ministers make better use of their time. When they understand what a great task is before them they will see how little time they have for relaxation.

13. It will bring us many personal benefits. It will stimulate our own spiritual growth and comfort us to know we have done our duty. Calling people to turn from their sins will make us watch ourselves more carefully. Telling them about the joys of heaven will quicken our own desires for glory. This is a far better way of promoting holiness than retreating into a monastery!

14. It will turn people's attention away from useless arguments. Turning their thoughts to the great essentials of Christianity will allow them less time for minor matters that contribute little to their growth in grace.

15. We will reach more people with the gospel. Not everyone will be converted, but, because more people will hear the gospel, we believe more will be saved. God's elect are scattered in the world and the gospel is the means of gathering them in. A systematic method of personal evangelism is much better than just talking to people when we have an opportunity. It is easier to press home the awfulness of sin and the need for conversion when we arrange to meet them for that purpose.

16. It will encourage many other ministers to begin this work. When they see the benefits of this work they will want to do it themselves. Many godly ministers are as uncertain about the

advantages as we were. When they see what an effective means it is of extending Christ's kingdom they will be encouraged to begin. Would it not be wonderful if every faithful pastor began this work!

17. Finally, this work is essential for the reformation of the church. It is a vital means of answering the fervent prayers of God's people and averting God's judgments.

If this work is neglected the church will remain in its present poor state. How can we claim to live for Christ and never deny ourselves or make any great efforts to serve Him? Are we only thinking about a revival sent from God and not a reformation to be laboured at ourselves? Are we hoping the Holy Spirit will come and thousands will be converted every time we preach? Do you not understand you must diligently work in earnest preaching and catechising regardless of the cost to yourselves?

Do you not realise that revival brings a far greater workload? Few realise how demanding it is until they are in the midst of it. Difficulties and oppositions will then test our resolve to the limit. When God sends revival it is often very different from our romantic expectations. Many ministers think revival will give them more influence and financial security. But they will find it demands more hard work and humility than ever and they will also have to abandon many false assumptions.

Article 2

Motives from the difficulties of the work
These would be discouragements on their own, but when seen alongside the benefits they should stimulate us to greater diligence.

1. Difficulties in ourselves:
    a) Our fallen nature makes us lazy and reluctant to work. We must make every effort to overcome this.
    b) We want to please people too much. Would we rather risk God's displeasure and people's salvation than warn them about hell and maybe lose their friendship? We should strongly resist this temptation.
    c) Many are too shy to speak to people about their need of Christ.
    d) We are too ready to yield to self-interest. We should not flinch at opposition or loss if we are to serve Christ faithfully.
    e) The greatest hindrance is our weakness of faith. Therefore, our witness to Christ often lacks certainty and conviction. We need to be well grounded in Scripture for our faith to be strong and vigorous.
    f) Finally, we often lack sufficient skill and ability for the work. Few understand how believers think or the best way of communicating the gospel to them. This is as least as difficult as preaching.
    g) We should not let these difficulties discourage us; rather they should inspire us to overcome them.

2. Difficulties with our people:
    a) (a) Some are too proud or stubborn or self-righteous to come for instruction. We need to persuade them it is in their best interests.
    b) (b) Many who are willing often have difficulties in learning. They will stop coming unless we encourage them.

c) (c) Many lack the necessary educational background to understand us unless we make our teaching very clear and plain.

d) (d) The greatest difficulty is to awaken their consciences. The heart of a sinner is rock hard. Your teaching will make no impression unless you are serious, earnest and persuasive. Only the Holy Spirit can awaken dead souls. However, he usually employs suitable means. He does not normally use ministers who are dull or worldly.

e) (e) Finally, even awakened sinners will soon return to their old ways unless they are properly nurtured and cared for.

Article 3

Motives from the necessity of the work

1. This duty is necessary for the glory of God. The purpose of our lives is to glorify God and so we should do that which will honour Him the most. If every pastor undertook this work and the Lord blessed their labours it would bring great glory to Christ. The foolish would become wise, sinners would be saved, God's people would be strengthened, the idle would become busy servants of Christ and God's Word would become the topic of conversation in every home and place of work. God would then live in our midst and Christ would be glorified in His saints.

Every Christian is obliged to do all they can for the salvation of sinners. This is especially true of ministers who have been set apart for this work. God has used personal teaching to bring many to salvation. If ministers examined their people they would see what little impression their preaching has made. I work hard to prepare my sermons and I preach as simply and fervently as possible. Yet some who seemed avid listeners for years hardly knew the basic truths about Christ. When I explained the gospel they seem astonished as if they never heard it before. I have found that many are more deeply affected by God's Word after half an hour's personal instruction than from ten years' preaching!

Preaching is the best method of evangelism because we can speak to more people. But personal instruction is more effective because it can be adapted to the needs of individuals. Many find it difficult to follow our sermons. In private we can teach gradually and find how much they understand from their answers. We can also help each individual with their particular difficulties.

2. This duty is necessary for the good of our people. Can you be a faithful pastor and fail to see your people's need? You have compassion on the homeless, the hungry, the sick and the dying. So why don't you have compassion on those living in sin and heading for judgment and hell? If you have compassion why not do this work for them?

There are multitudes of sinners around you and your voice is the appointed means of awakening them. If someone seeking salvation begged your assistance would you not leave your studies to help them? Yet those who reject your help are the most needy. They are unaware of their spiritual misery and danger. Can you converse light-heartedly with unbelievers knowing their miserable state? Should you not weep over them, earnestly beseeching them to turn to Christ? Therefore rouse yourself and spare no effort that might contribute to their salvation.

3. This work is for your own benefit as well as your people's. You will have to give an account of your ministry before Christ's judgment seat. If you fail to warn unbelievers, God has promised, 'his blood I will require at your hand'. There is a day coming when many will regret they ever entered the ministry. Besides their own sins they will have the blood of many souls to answer for. How wonderful if we can then say, 'I lived for Christ not myself; I showed people their sins and declared the way of salvation.' If you want to die well and enjoy an eternal reward, then stir yourself to do those works that please Christ.

Article 4

The application of these motives

1. How greatly we should be humbled before God today for neglecting the personal instruction of those entrusted to our care. God alone knows how many we could have helped. Why did we not begin sooner? There are many hindrances: Satan, sin-hardened hearts, etc... However, the greatest hindrance is in ourselves: our unbelief, dividedness, dullness and aversion to work. Our guilt is so great because the work we have neglected is so vital. We have no excuse. We can only plead God's mercy. May He wash our guilt in the blood of Christ and turn His anger from us. We have days of national humiliation because of God's judgments on the sins of our nation. May every pastor in this country hold a day of humiliation for the sins of the ministry. We should all lay aside pride, contentiousness, self-ambition and slothfulness lest God should lay us aside.

2. Brethren, from now on let us deny ourselves and get to work. The harvest is great and the labourers few. Souls are precious and the plight of sinners is great. It is no small honour to be Christ's fellow worker. We have wasted too much time already. Multitudes are speeding to hell. Are these thoughts not enough to awaken you to your duty? We cannot awaken others if we are drowsy ourselves. What does it take to convince you of your responsibilities? Should not one verse of Scripture be enough? Should not the pathetic sight of your godless neighbours be sufficient persuasion?

O that we were more deeply convinced of the truth so that we could convince others. What an improvement that would make to our lives and our ministry! I often wonder why my preaching is so cold and superficial when people are so careless about their sin and the coming judgment. I seldom leave the pulpit without feeling guilty because I have not been sufficiently serious and fervent. My conscience asks, 'How could you speak of heaven and hell so casually? Do you really believe what you are saying? How can you describe the misery of sin and fail to be moved? Should you not weep over these people? Should you not raise your voice and plead with them as for life and death?'

May the Lord deliver us from unfaithfulness and hardness of heart that we may be fit instruments for saving others. If you had faced death as often as I have, your conscience would be keener. It often asks me, 'Is this all your concern for the lost? Why do you not do more for their salvation? How many will be in hell before you speak to them?' I seldom hear the funeral bell tolling without asking myself, 'What have you done to prepare that soul for judgment?' We can easily brush aside such questions now. However, the day is coming when it will not be conscience, but Christ who will be asking these questions.

I have no wish to cause unnecessary anxiety. However, it may help us to consider the day of judgment, especially to think of those who will rise up to accuse unfaithful ministers.

a) Our parents will condemn us saying, 'Lord, we devoted them to your service, but they despised it and served themselves.'

b) Our teachers will accuse us because the whole purpose of our studies was to equip us for serving Christ.

c) Our abilities and knowledge will condemn us because we failed to use them faithfully in our ministry.

d) Our ministerial ambitions will condemn us because we were unfaithful to our trust.

e) God's love for His people will accuse us because we neglected souls for whom Christ died.

f) The commands of Scripture will condemn us because we failed to take them seriously.

g) The prophets and apostles will accuse us because we failed to follow their example of faithfulness in the ministry.

h) The Bible and our books will condemn us because we did not use them as we should.

i) Our own sermons will condemn us because we failed to practise ourselves what we preached to others.

j) All our wages will accuse us. We received financial support in order to give ourselves fully to our work and not to be idle and self-indulgent.

k) Our criticisms of negligent ministers will return upon us if we are also unfaithful.

l) God's judgments against unfaithful ministers will condemn us. Some have lost God's blessing or their reputations or they have been dismissed from the ministry. If we fail to heed these warnings our condemnation will be greater.

m) Finally, all the fervent prayers of God's people for reformation and revival will rise up and accuse us. Few nations have had so much prayer offered for them both publicly and privately. Is it not hypocrisy if we pray much and then ignore our responsibilities for evangelism and exercising church discipline? Some Christians say they long for revival, but when it comes to ordering their lives according to God's Word their longing seems to evaporate! I have often heard men pray and preach fervently for church discipline but in practice they refuse to do it!

Experience often demonstrates our pitiful weakness. We have avoided many aspects of our work requiring painful decisions and self-sacrifice. Yet Christ is wonderfully patient with us. O that our hearts were broken and we were resolved to neglect our duties no longer. Let us be determined to love and obey Christ whatever labours and sufferings that may involve, even if it means death.

I have explained what will happen if we refuse to serve Christ faithfully. We are under a great obligation to be diligent and neglect will bring condemnation. I would not have been so outspoken if our calling were not so vital to ourselves, our people and to the glory of God. We cannot moderate our speech when dealing with matters of eternal life and death. There are many things in the church we would like to change, but leading sinners to Christ and building up the saints is the very essence of our work.

Now brethren, the work lies before you. You must preach and teach in public and in private. You should easily perceive what a great work this is. If you value your leisure time more than precious souls then just stick to preaching. But if not, you should get to work!

Section 3. Answers to Objections

1. If we teach our people in public it is unnecessary to teach them privately as well.

Answer: The apostle Paul taught both 'in public and from house to house' (Acts 20:20). Many who listened to my clear preaching for many years were amazingly ignorant of basic Christianity. But after an hour's private teaching they understood more than in all their lives before.

2. We are only responsible for those in our congregations.

Answer: We are commanded to bring the gospel to as many as possible and this is one of the most effective ways of doing it.

3. This work is so demanding we will have no time for proper study.

Answer:

    a) Ministers should already be well grounded in doctrine and able to teach others what they know. The salvation of lost souls is more important than study.

    b) Teaching the fundamentals of Christianity will deepen your understanding of them. You may not learn so many less essential truths, but your knowledge will be the best in the world. Time spent in this work provides invaluable experience and is very beneficial to your people.

c) Nevertheless, because study is so valuable, I recommend you give it as much time as possible. If we reduce time-wasting we can surely find enough time for catechising our people as well as for study.

d) If time is short we should get our priorities right and concentrate on the most essential duties. I would rather give up all my books than be guilty of the loss of one soul.

4. We would wear ourselves out with continual work. We need time for relaxation and companionship.

Answer:

a) This is an argument for the self-indulgent and lazy. If everyone thought like that there would have been no martyrs, nor indeed any Christians!

b) We have enough time for recreation without neglecting our duty. My poor health means I need more exercise than most and an hour's walk before lunch is enough for me. If anyone thinks they need much more they should reconsider the need to deny themselves. If the apostle needed to keep his body under subjection how much more do we? Anyone who loves pleasure so much he cannot make sacrifices to speak to perishing souls is unfit for the ministry.

c) What is our time and energy for but to be spent for God? As a candle is made for burning, so it is better to burn ourselves out shedding light on the way of salvation than in living for pleasure.

d) Are your friends and family more important than your ministry? Will you neglect your duty to spend more time with them? Will you honour them before

God? If you are still trying to please men you are no
servant of Christ.

I cannot understand ministers spending hours in leisure
activities when so many souls are perishing around them. If
you do not appreciate the value of souls or the greatness of
Christ's sacrifice for them you are unfit for the ministry. Time
is precious. The years pass swiftly away. Have you not already
wasted enough time on trivialities? If others can waste their
time on excessive recreation, we cannot. Can a doctor relax
when surrounded by the sick and dying? Can a soldier relax
in the heat of battle? Their duties involve issues of life and
death, but ours involve eternity.

5. I do not think God would burden us with the extra
responsibility of teaching everyone individually.
Answer: We have already shown that this work is both essential
and clearly commanded. Can we sit back while sinners rush to
damnation because it is too burdensome to help them? Is that
compassion or laziness? Do you only obey God when it pleases
you? Do you honour God by calling His work drudgery? Are
you fit to be a minister of Christ, if you are not prepared to
deny yourself?

It is tragic that so many ministers are unconverted and have
not the Spirit of Christ. Jesus went without dinner to speak to
one woman. Do you really believe in heaven and hell? If you
do, how can you think any effort to save the lost is excessive?
Do you not realise you are denying yourself a blessing? It is
one of those strange mysteries of the Christian life that the
more you give the more you receive. When we obey Christ
we experience more of His love, joy and peace. Grace grows
by exercise. To those who use their talents diligently Christ

has promised an eternal reward. Is that a 'burden'? Pastoral neglect is a terrible sin, but will you aggravate your sin by making excuses for it?

6. New Testament times were very different from our own. Pastors then had the great task of founding the church in the face of intense persecution.

Answer: Those who make this objection are out of touch with reality. Is there really such a shortage of hypocrites in the church and all kinds of sinners in the world that we can relax our efforts? Is our age really that much better than previous ones because people are now more educated and advanced? We only need to look at the state of the church and the world around us to see the absurdity of this objection.

7. If we make the work too demanding men will be reluctant to enter the ministry and there will be a shortage of ministers.

Answer:

    a) These demands on the ministry are not ours but Christ's. Why should God relieve us of our responsibilities and allow our neighbours to perish?

    b) Christ has not suffered so much for the church to leave her without ministers. It is He who raises up men for the work and equips them with His Spirit. Christ has promised to provide 'pastors after his own heart' who will gladly 'endure all things for the sake of his elect'. We will often fail in our duty and we continually need Christ's forgiveness. However, refusing to enter the ministry because it is too demanding is a deliberate and serious sin.

8. If most people reject our teaching it is a pointless exercise.

Answer:

    a)   There are indeed many obstinate people, but that itself shows the seriousness of their condition. We must therefore work harder to persuade them.

    b)   Much of our people's opposition is due to our lack of zeal and consistency. Some good preachers are so arrogant it puts people off.

    c)   Our people's lack of enthusiasm does not excuse our own. Those who reject our ministry increase their guilt. If we refuse to do our duty we will be held guilty.

    d)   Those who reject our ministry allow us to spend more time with those who accept it and so they will benefit all the more.

9. If preaching is the main method God has given for the conversion of sinners, why is it necessary to teach them individually?

Answer:

    a)   Counselling individuals will help us understand our people better. This in turn will help our sermon preparation.

    b)   Whether we are speaking to thousands or to one, it is still preaching. There is nothing unreasonable or unscriptural about teaching individuals. We have many examples in the Bible. The only opposition comes from sin and Satan, but God will give us grace to overcome.

We can learn a great deal from our text (Acts 20:18-33, kjv):

- Our overall duty: 'serving the LORD with all humility'.

- Our particular task: 'Take heed to yourselves and to all the flock'.
- Our teaching: 'repentance toward God, and faith in our Lord Jesus Christ'.
- The method: 'I … have taught you publicly, and from house to house'.
- His love and zeal: 'I ceased not to warn everyone night and day with tears'.
- His faithfulness: 'I kept back nothing that was profitable to you … I have not shunned to declare unto you the whole counsel of God'.
- His self-denial: 'I have coveted no one's silver or gold or apparel'.
- His patience and perseverance: 'none of these things move me'.
- His prayerfulness: 'I commend you to God, and to the word of his grace'.
- His purity of motive: 'Wherefore I take you to record this day, that I am innocent of the blood of all men'.

If we memorised these verses and meditated on them it would help us to be better ministers. Remember the one thing needful: 'seek first the kingdom of God and his righteousness'. The sincere pastor has God's glory and the salvation of souls as his constant aim. This lightens the burden of our work and makes our sufferings worthwhile. God will never allow anyone to be a loser by serving Him. Christ's faithful servants will receive a reward that will more than compensate for any loss. Need I say more to convince you to be fully committed to the work?

Section 4 . The Management of Personal Work

Article 1

We need to ensure we teach as many as possible

1. It is vital that people are convinced of their pastor's ability and love for them. If his ability is suspect they will not value his teaching. If the sincerity of his love is questionable they will not trust him. But if they are assured of his ability and love they will respect his advice.

If ministers tried harder to win people's affection their ministry would be more effective. If we face opposition through no fault of our own, we must continue teaching with patience and humility. If we are at fault we must try our best to put things right. If people still oppose us, it may be best to leave and let someone else try to help them.

2. Having gained people's love and respect, we must then show them the benefits of personal instruction. Preach some relevant sermons before you begin. Stress their need to grow spiritually and to serve the Lord. For example, you could show them, from Hebrews 5:12:

  a) They must learn from God's Word and ministers are appointed to teach them.

  b) They first need to know the fundamentals without which they can neither be saved nor make progress in their faith.

c) Convince them, especially those who have attended for many years, of their need to benefit from the ministry. If not, they have to be taught again no matter how old they are. We cannot be Christians unless we receive Christ's teaching. If they reject their pastor's teaching they are, in effect, rejecting Christ.

People must understand that our role as their teacher is a responsibility God has given us. Explain our duties towards them and their own duty of submitting to our teaching.

3. After persuading them of their need of teaching you must provide every family with a catechism. Some would not bother to buy one themselves and giving them one will make them feel some obligation to use it. It is best to distribute them yourself. You can then encourage them to learn it and make a note of all those old enough to learn. The expense should be met by the church. You could hold a special service and have an offering dedicated to the work. After allowing them enough time to learn their catechism you need to see them family by family.

4. Treat them gently and encourage them as much as possible.
   a) It does not matter if they have already learned another catechism. The teachings of all orthodox catechisms are basically the same.
   b) Older people who have difficulty remembering the words should be told not to worry as long as they understand the meaning.
   c) If the first families you see are greatly helped this will encourage the others to come.

Finally, you should revisit those who reject your teaching. Find the reason for their opposition and warn them that such stubbornness is sinful. Souls are too precious to give up without trying our utmost to help them.

Article 2

How to work effectively

Catechising is not as easy as you may think. Teaching an unbeliever basic Christianity is more demanding than preaching and more difficult than theological debate! Unless we firmly lay the foundation of the doctrine of Christ the rest of our work will be ineffective.

1.Begin with an explanation of the reasons for the work and its necessity for their salvation and Christian growth. This will encourage your people to be responsive to your teaching.

2. Next, speak to each one in private. If they feel embarrassed before others because they cannot answer correctly they will not want to continue. They will also feel very uncomfortable talking about their sins and their problems unless they are alone with you. However, someone else should always be present when you are speaking with women. A suitable member of her family could be present. That would minimise the risk of embarrassment if you are overheard. With the most antagonistic we need to speak firmly. If we are then overheard it might benefit others also. Attention to detail is very important. Small mistakes can create great hindrances.

3. Begin by finding how much of the catechism they have learned. If they have difficulty, encourage them to learn at least the Apostles' Creed and the Ten Commandments.

4. Find out how much they understand of the most important truths. Carefully note the following points:

a) Begin by questioning them on those issues they believe are most relevant to themselves. Ask them questions such as, 'What will happen to you after you die?', 'What is the penalty for sin?', 'What is God's remedy for sin?', etc...

b) Avoid questions that are unnecessary or difficult to answer. Be careful about questions such as 'What is God?' or 'What is faith?' Many ministers find it difficult to answer such questions properly. It is possible to have a sound understanding and a genuine experience without being able to explain them clearly.

c) Make your questions as clear as possible. Let them understand you only require a simple response in their own words. If they do not understand, you could frame your questions in a way that only requires a simple 'Yes' or 'No' answer. For example, 'What is God. Is he an invisible Spirit?'

d) We need to be careful in our interpretation of their answers. For example, they may say we need to repent in order to be forgiven. That could mean they are still trusting their own efforts rather than the finished work of Christ. We will sometimes need to question them further to find out exactly what they do mean. Some may have a saving knowledge of Christ but have difficulty expressing it. Some godly old believers will tearfully confess their inability to learn the catechism. When you consider all the Bible teaching and fellowship they have enjoyed for many years it shows how dull Christians can be. This should make us cautious lest we too hastily dismiss such people as unbelievers.

e) Those who are completely unable to answer our questions need to have the basics explained to them again. They may then understand the answers to the questions before the interview is over.

5. Having discovered how much they know, continue to teach them what they need to learn next. This will vary according to each individual, maybe a better understanding of the gospel or some duties they are unsure about. If they know very little you should give them a brief summary of basic Christianity in ordinary language. Close with a brief application. If they still do not understand, go over it again and fix it in their memories.

6. If you think they may be unconverted, describe some of the marks of true conversion and ask them whether they have experienced this great change in their soul. Try to avoid giving offence by explaining the vital importance of this question. Ask them these questions:

a) Do they feel the guilt and burden of their sins? Do they realise they deserve eternal condemnation? Have they trusted Christ alone for forgiveness?

b) Do they hate their former sins? Are they willing to deny themselves so they can live to please God?

c) Are they willing to give up everything in the world for Christ? Although often troubled by sin and failure, is it their greatest desire to please God and enjoy Him forever?

If they can honestly give positive answers to these questions, remind them of the great privilege of being a Christian. Then highlight areas of their lives that need attention such as keeping Sundays holy or family devotions.

7. If, however, you have good reason to believe they are unconverted then, as tactfully as possible, draw attention to their tragic state. Show them how they have wasted their time, living for themselves, indifferent to their spiritual needs. Remind them of the uncertainty of life and where they will go if they die in their sins. You should be gentle but forthright in speaking to them. If your words make little impression they will soon be forgotten.

8. Conclude by setting two duties before them:
   a) The need to mourn for their sins and receive Christ as Lord and Saviour. They must not be content until God gives them a new heart to love Him and to hate sin. Contrast the emptiness of this world's pleasures with the eternal glory of heaven. Emphasise their need to come to the Saviour without delay and to receive the free gift of pardon and eternal life. Tell them to turn away from all sin as they would avoid deadly poison.
   b) They should diligently use the means of grace until they are converted and established in their faith.
       • Since God alone can cause this change they must continually pray for forgiveness and a new heart.

- They should avoid ungodly company and make friends with God's people. They should also avoid temptation and break sinful habits.
- They should use Sundays to seek the Lord in private and in public worship. God has especially given us this day to seek Him and to prepare ourselves for eternity. Have them solemnly promise before God to do these things as much as they possibly can.

9. Before they leave, give them some words of encouragement. Remind them that all these duties are essential for their eternal benefit.

When you see them again, encourage them to carry on. The head of each family should gather everyone together to learn the catechism on Sundays. After learning it they should continue to go through it in case they forget. Those living alone could find a suitable person amongst their neighbours to help them.

10. Keep a record of all your people and make a note of the day you catechised them. Record the names of those fit to receive Communion. Also note those who oppose instruction and treat them as if they had excommunicated themselves.

11. Conduct the whole interview in a proper manner.
   a) Deal with each individual in a way that is appropriate to their character. Young people should be warned about sensual sins and advised about resisting them. Remind older people they need to be prepared to leave this world. Warn rich people against trusting their wealth and show them their need of self-sacrifice.

Remind the poor of their riches in Christ. Warn women against gossiping, men against drunkenness and ambition, etc…

b) Be sympathetic, friendly and patient with those who are slow-witted.

c) Support everything you say with Scripture so they can see you are not speaking on your own behalf but God's.

d) Be as earnest as possible throughout the interview, especially when giving practical advice. A cold, formal approach will achieve little. Remember how precious souls are and be serious as in a matter of life and death.

e) It is essential to prepare our hearts beforehand. We should realise the awesomeness of the eternal issues we are dealing with. You cannot get away with an affected fervency as easily as in a pulpit which is a hypocrite's stage! Only sincere fervency will do for this work. You cannot press home the truth without it.

f) Prepare your hearts beforehand in private prayer. If you have time, open and close in prayer with them.

g) In all our counselling we should constantly assure them of our loving concern. Avoid language that is harsh or discouraging.

h) If you are short of time, concentrate on the most essential things. If there are close and trusted friends you could interview them together. Then see them separately to deal with the most sensitive issues and practical directions. However, make sure you do not rush the interview.

i) Finally, if you can, recompense the poorest for their lost wages because of time spent with you, particularly those who have tried their best

That concludes my advice, so I will now leave you to get on with your task. I am sure God will use this exhortation to awaken many of his servants to their duty, despite the opposition of sin and Satan. We pray that God will bless this work, save many souls, give you much encouragement and build His church. *Amen.*

Painting of the Kidderminster church in older times

Baxter statue outside Kidderminster church today

Richard Baxter's house in the High Street, Kidderminster, before alterations in 1848. Notice the basket makerworking in the cellar. Richard Baxter rented the first and second floors of the house, the ground floor being occupied by a cobbler.

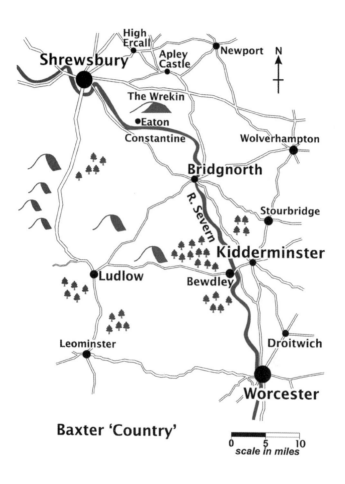

Baxter 'country'

The Life of
Richard Baxter
1615 – 1691

W. Stuart Owen

Contents

Introduction

Almost a hundred years before Richard Baxter was born, Tyndale's Bible was being smuggled into England. The rediscovery of the Bible, following many centuries of neglect, was the means of bringing the light of the gospel of Christ into the spiritual darkness of England. That same light revealed the corruption of the established church. This awakened, in many, a burning desire to cleanse the church from all the superstitious beliefs and ceremonies accumulated during the centuries of Papal domination. These men were known as the Reformers, and later as the Puritans.[1] The power struggle between Reformation and Counter-Reformation reached its climax during Baxter's lifetime. Baxter was deeply involved in many aspects of this great conflict. He preached before both Charles II and Cromwell and courageously reproved them for their sins. He witnessed the horrors of the Civil War, the Plague and the Great Fire of London. He bore with dignity the malicious insults of the notorious Judge Jeffries. Baxter was a man who could not be bought with a bribe or silenced by threats or prison. During his lifetime he brushed with death so frequently he called it his 'friend'. However, by the grace of God, he lived to see, in the 'Glorious Revolution' of 1688, the downfall of his persecutors. During an era which Milton described as one of 'sects and schisms', Baxter promoted the cause of unity between true believers.

---

1. The term 'Puritan' was originally used as an insult against those who sought to live consistently according to the Bible, very much as 'Methodist' was used in the 18th Century. 'Precisian' was another common nickname used to describe the Puritans. The insult lay in the connotations of censoriousness, aloofness, hypocrisy and spiritual pride conveyed by these terms.

Even though Baxter was born in Shropshire and spent most of his life elsewhere, his name has always been closely associated with the town of Kidderminster. The reason for this is the extraordinary measure of blessing that attended his ministry in that place. Both the Bible and history demonstrate that such a measure of blessing is almost invariably related to the means employed. There are particular truths and certain methods that God is pleased to bless far above all others.

While we do not believe Baxter was right in everything, he was accepted as a Puritan leader within the mainstream of Reformed tradition. Moreover, he learned from experience that the most profitable truths were not the finer details of theology but the great essential teachings of Christianity. He said, 'My Religion is meerly Christian.'[2] His basic theology, his belief in the verbal inspiration and authority of the Bible, the nature of Christ as perfect God and man, His death on the cross to pay the penalty for sin, God's gracious gift of faith to his elect, man's responsibility to repent and believe the gospel, and so on, are all considered as 'outmoded' by many leaders in the modern church. However, I believe it would be foolish to allow such an assertion to remain unchallenged. Surely the real value of any religion depends firstly on its truth and, secondly, its effectiveness in bringing people back to God. If modern theology really is so superior, then why is it so ineffective in bringing sinners to Christ? Like Baxter, we believe that nothing even remotely approaches biblical Christianity in its power to transform a life crippled by sin and guilt into one of real holiness and joy. This was the case not only three hundred years ago, but also in Britain in the 1990's. Baxter's tender conscience and his continual living near to death gave him

---

2. A phrase later adopted by C.S. Lewis as the title for his book 'Mere Christianity'.

a lively awareness of the awful danger of spiritual delusion. He was only able to overcome doubts about the genuineness of his faith after much inner struggle. This deep concern for spiritual realism spilled over into his ministry and explains why he preached and laboured with such tremendous zeal and fervour, as 'a dying man to dying men'.

Over a hundred years ago, one of Baxter's biographers wrote, 'It is impossible to doubt that Puritanism produced the freedom, strength and activity of modern British and American life. We owe our liberty, our power of social organisation, our ideas of the propriety and dignity of public virtue and of private purity, to the resistance our forefathers made to the tyranny and immorality of the Stuart dynasty.'[3] In 1925 a new biography of Richard Baxter appeared which attracted the attention of Dr Martyn Lloyd-Jones, from which time he dated his 'true and living interest in the Puritans and their works'.[4] This eventually led to the initiation of the annual Puritan Conference in 1950 (since renamed the Westminster Conference) and which continues to this day. It is my desire that many others, in our day, will catch something of Baxter's vision, zeal for God and love for the souls of men. May God help us to learn from these great men of the past the lessons they themselves so painfully learned.

---

3. J.H. Davies.
4. See Dr D.M. Lloyd-Jones, 'Puritanism and its Origins', *The Good Fight of Faith* (1971 Westminster Conference Report), London, 1972, p. 71.

Nothing so little as grace at first, and nothing more glorious afterward: things of greatest perfection are longest in coming to their growth ...

A new creature [in Christ] is the most excellent frame in all the world, therefore it groweth up by degrees; we see in nature, that a mighty oak riseth of an acorn.

(From *The Bruised Reed* by Richard Sibbes)

Chapter 1. The Formative Years

Richard Baxter was born in Rowton, Shropshire, on Sunday, 12 November 1615 at the time of morning worship. His parents, Richard and Beatrice Baxter, were freehold farmers in the village of Eaton Constantine, between the Wrekin Hill and the River Severn. At the time of their son's birth they were impoverished due to gambling debts incurred by Richard senior during his youth. As a result, Richard Baxter had to spend much of his boyhood living with his maternal grandfather in Rowton, near High Ercall, about ten miles away, until he was nearly ten years old.

In those days there was little opportunity to hear gospel preaching in Shropshire. However, about the time of his son's birth, Richard senior was converted through reading the Bible. One of the results of this was that he later sought to influence his son with the truths of Scripture. 'When I was very young', says Baxter, 'his serious speeches of God and the life to come possessed me with a fear of sinning'. His father encouraged him to read the historical books of the Bible. He enjoyed these very much, and eventually he began to appreciate the more doctrinal portions of the Bible as well.

On Sundays, the family would spend time together reading the Bible or devotional books and singing God's praises. However, their devotions were often disturbed by the sounds of revelry and dancing as the villagers gathered around the nearby maypole. Young Richard was often tempted to join them, and sometimes he did. However, when he heard his father being 'derided ... under the odious name of Puritan', he joined them no more. This incident brought home to him the great contrast between his father's uprightness and the godlessness of those who sneered at him.

His godly upbringing gave young Baxter a troubled conscience whenever he indulged in the usual boyish sins. Of these he lists the following: lying to escape punishment; eating too many apples and pears; stealing fruit from orchards; playing too much; gambling; being over fond of reading romances and old fables; imitating other boys in their foolish talking and behaviour; being over fond of his teacher's praises; and being cheeky and disrespectful towards his parents. These, he says, were not overcome without a long struggle. However, he later said that he found, even in childhood, 'a Power to awe my soul and to check my sin and folly'.

Richard Baxter loved the beautiful countryside of his native Shropshire. 'When I was a boy' he wrote, 'I was wont to go up the Wrekin Hill with great pleasure (being near my dwelling) and to look down on the country below me and see the villages as little things'. It was during his early teens that he encountered the first of many narrow escapes from death. He was riding a shire horse in a field near his home when it suddenly bolted towards a hedge behind which was a drop of about fifteen feet into a narrow lane. Richard was thrown off and landed in the soft mud of the lane. The horse landed on top of him — on all fours — with two feet on either side!

Richard excelled in school. He was very bright and was never satisfied until he had mastered any subject he studied. He acknowledged the great help and encouragement he received from John Owen, schoolmaster of Wroxeter free school (not the famous Puritan of the same name). Whilst in Wroxeter, Richard stayed in the home of Sir Richard (later Lord) Newport, and attended school with his sons. Another of his fellow pupils was Richard Allestree, who later became Regius Professor of Divinity at Oxford, and Provost of Eton College. Naturally, these two Richards were keen academic rivals. It was customary in those days for the ablest students to be given some responsibility for teaching the younger pupils. This had been Baxter's privilege until, one day, Mr Owen gave this position to his rival. Baxter was so upset by this that he felt like leaving the school altogether. However, he says that Mr Owen, thereupon, 'gravely, but very tenderly rebuked my pride, and gave me for my theme: "Ne sutor ultra crepidam"' *(Let the cobbler stick to his last).* In other words, 'Do not think more highly of yourself than you should!'

About the same time as this incident, when he was fifteen, Richard Baxter experienced a spiritual awakening. His conscience was stirred even more than usual, especially about his habit of raiding orchards, and he came under a conviction of sin.[1] He found much help and comfort through reading devotional books by the earlier Puritan authors. In particular he mentions one that his father had bought from a poor pedlar

---

1. A book that helped him to see the awfulness of sin was *'Bunny's Resolution'*. This was originally written by a Jesuit called Parsons, but which had been 'cleansed' of its Romanist sentiments by Edmund Bunny.

who had come to their door. This was 'Dr. Sibbes *Bruised Reed*', which he said was 'suited to my state and seasonably sent me ... He opened up more the love of God to me and gave me a livelier apprehension of the Mystery of Redemption and how much I am beholden to Jesus Christ'. Although he was never sure exactly when he was converted, Baxter traced his spiritual awakening to this time.

Baxter's ambition of going to university was never fulfilled. He was persuaded instead to become assistant to Mr Wickstead, Chaplain to the Council at Ludlow, and a friend of Mr Owen, Richard's teacher. He was led to believe that he would receive better than a university education with Mr Wickstead as his personal tutor. As it turned out, Mr Wickstead, although very fond of Richard, never taught him at all! However, he did allow Richard all the books and the time he wanted to teach himself.

In those days, Ludlow was an important regional administrative centre for much of Wales and the Marches. Richard found it to be a 'town ... full of temptations'. At one time he tried his hand at gambling and took some lessons from the foremost gambler in town. Whilst throwing the dice, Baxter had amazing 'luck'. He was shocked and believed the devil had taken control of the dice to lure him into habitual gambling. He immediately resolved never to gamble again. He records, with thankfulness, that God gave him a friend whose example of zeal and practical godliness was a great help. Together they would often walk and talk, read and pray. This friend was the first person he heard pray naturally (without reading out of a prayer book) and Richard soon learned to follow his example. However, it came as a great shock to Richard when, some time later, this friend fell into profanity and drunkenness. Baxter later wrote,

For such a friend I had, though after all
Himself became my warning by his fall.

After spending about eighteen months in Ludlow, Baxter returned to Eaton Constantine. He was dismayed to find his old teacher, Mr Owen, suffering with tuberculosis, from which he later died. Lord Newport asked Richard to teach in his place, which he did for a few months. However, he too began to show symptoms of the same terrible disease, which was incurable in those days. For quite some time he lived with the expectation that he was going to die. Doubts about the genuineness of his faith troubled him for many years. He gives three main reasons for these doubts:

Firstly, he could not reconcile his experience with the descriptions of conversion given in books on the subject, such as *Repentance* by William Perkins.

Secondly, he was disturbed by the fact that spiritual truths did not stir his emotions or grip his imagination as much as he felt they should.

Thirdly, he was concerned about the possibility that his faith was merely an intellectual understanding coupled with a fear of God, and that he was not truly regenerate.

However, he gradually came to see that his fear of God was beneficial because it kept him from falling into sin. Although his love was faint, it was, nevertheless, genuine and he really did love God, His Word and His people. He also learned not to place too much reliance on his senses and feelings. The Holy Spirit works firstly through the understanding and the emotions must follow. Also, God deals with different people in different ways as He sees fit. In later years, when he was in the position of having to counsel others he found that these doubts were quite common, and in answering their doubts he answered his own as well!

In the meantime, both his doubts and his fear of death caused him to become even more serious and resolute in seeking 'first ... God's Kingdom and his righteousness'. His main purpose in all his studies became, as he says, that of 'informing and reforming my own Soul'. All other studies he made subservient to that end. Therefore, his main studies were amongst the great wealth of practical and devotional literature written by the earlier Puritan authors. He also delighted in studying the writings of scholastics such as Thomas Aquinas and Duns Scotus. By adopting this method of study he wasted less time and it also enabled him to learn more efficiently. The only disadvantage of this method of study he found was that he was never able to master the biblical languages of Greek and Hebrew. This was a handicap that he never found time to remedy later on in life.[2]

Although Baxter did not die of tuberculosis, it nevertheless left him with much bodily weakness and pain for the remainder of his life. He was afflicted with a tubercular cough from time to time, and also nasal haemorrhaging. He was especially troubled by pain in his kidneys, which he believed was due to kidney stones 'occasioned by unsuitable diet in my youth'. Nevertheless, he was thankful to God that in all his life he was never overcome by depression, and that, despite his almost continual pain, it never seriously hindered him in his work, his study or his preaching.

---

2. Baxter's method of study may help to explain why his most valuable contribution to our spiritual heritage was to be his practical rather than his doctrinal works. His method of interpreting Scripture seems to have been influenced by the Scholastics and sometimes tended to be more rational and logical than exegetical.

Richard Baxter ... drew more hearts to the great Broken Heart than any single Englishman of his age.

Prof. Alexander Balloch Grosart

Chapter 2. The Ministry

Baxter's father believed that his son had been 'consecrated from the womb' to be God's spokesman, after the pattern of the biblical prophets. Even as a young boy, if he heard other children use bad language he would reprove them in a way that amazed those who heard him. However, when he was about eighteen years old, Baxter was almost persuaded, by Mr Wickstead of Ludlow, to abandon his ambition of entering the ministry. He was advised that his best chances for advancement lay in spending time at the royal court and seeking some government office. Richard's parents also liked this proposal as they had doubts about their son entering the Christian ministry. However, Baxter's experience of court was not a happy one. 'When I saw a stage-play instead of a sermon on the Lord's days ... and heard little preaching but what was ... against the Puritans, I was glad to be gone'. After just a month in the Palace at Whitehall, Richard's mother fell ill and wanted to see him. He was glad of an excuse to leave the corrupt court of Charles I, and resolved never to return.

The winter of 1633/34 was the worst in living memory. The snow lasted from Christmas until Easter. Kidderminster was completely cut off. In desperation, some men tried to dig their way through to Stourbridge to get coal for heating. Whilst on their way a blizzard struck and some were trapped and froze to death. Baxter, on his way home to Shropshire from London, also narrowly missed death. His horse slipped and threw him under the wheels of a cart. For some unaccountable reason the horses drawing the cart stopped just inches short of crushing him to death. On 10 May 1634 Baxter's mother died in great pain.

When he was in his early twenties Baxter felt so ill that he expected to die soon. The recurring bouts of illness made him feel he was continually living on the brink of eternity. This made him see the great urgency of persuading 'such ignorant, presumptuous and careless sinners as the world aboundeth with' to repent and believe in Christ. It was at this time that he first met some Nonconformist pastors from Shrewsbury and was impressed and helped by the 'fervent prayers, godly conversation and holiness' of their lives. This contact made him study the issue of conformity to the established church. He concluded that, although there were some practices of the Anglican Church with which he disagreed,[1] he nevertheless felt the weight of argument was in favour of conformity. Thus, when Richard Baxter was offered the position of schoolmaster at Dudley,[2] he accepted and was ordained by the Bishop of Worcester on Advent Sunday 1638. Dudley also presented Baxter with opportunities for public preaching. He describes the people as poor and 'famous for drunkenness' but also teachable and ready to receive God's Word. Baxter had only spent nine months in Dudley when he accepted an invitation to Bridgnorth as curate to the vicar, Mr Madstart, whom he

---

1. Such as the wearing of surplices, the sign of the cross in baptism and the lack of any meaningful form of church discipline.
2. A new school built by Mr Richard Foley of Stourbridge.

describes as a 'good preacher and a most excellent minister'. However, Baxter found the people, apart from some notable exceptions, to be rather apathetic and unresponsive to the gospel.

About this time the power struggle between King Charles I and Parliament began to increase. Two issues produced a great deal of agitation in the country. One was the 'ship money' controversy, which was the question whether the King had the authority to raise taxes without the permission of Parliament. The other was the 'Etcetera Oath' in which all clergy were required to swear not to seek the overthrow of the bishops. Baxter believed the debate produced by this controversial oath alienated more people from the bishops than if the question had never been raised. Upon examining the issue for himself, Baxter concluded that the episcopal system, as then constituted, was 'guilty of corrupting both churches and clergy'.

In 1640, Parliament, with the agreement of Charles I, appointed a committee to investigate complaints against clergy. The aim was to remove persons who were unfit to be ministers of religion either because of incompetence or scandalous behaviour. Amongst the many petitions immediately received was one from the people of Kidderminster. The vicar was so incompetent that he had become an object of common ridicule. He also frequented alehouses and was sometimes drunk. His curate was also incompetent, a drunkard and made some extra income during the week by conducting illicit marriages. However, Mr Danse, the vicar, was quite shrewd and was able to come to an agreement with Sir Henry Herbert,[3] the presenter of the petition. According to the deal,

3. Henry was the brother of George Herbert the preacher and hymnwriter. Henry was a member of Parliament for Bewdley, which was an important trading centre in those days about three miles west of Kidderminster.

the vicar would retain his position, but the curate could be replaced by a preacher to be chosen by the town's fourteen trustees. The first candidate, a Mr Lapthorn, was a well-known preacher. However, they were put off by his rambling and disorganised sermon. The next candidate, Richard Baxter, was unanimously chosen the first time they heard him preach.

Baxter was drawn to the people of Kidderminster as much as they were drawn to him. He says, 'My mind was much to the place as soon as it was described to me, because it was a full congregation ... an ignorant, rude and revelling people for the greater part, who had need of preaching, and yet had among them a small company of converts, who were humble, godly and of good conversations, and not much hated by the rest, and therefore fitter to assist their teacher; but above all, because they hardly ever had any lively, serious preaching among them. For Bridgnorth had made me resolve that I would never more go among a people that had been hardened in unprofitableness under an awakening ministry ... And thus I was brought, by the gracious providence of God, to that place which had the chiefest of my labours and yielded me the greatest fruits of comfort'.

Chapter 3. The Civil War

When Richard Baxter first came to Kidderminster he did not have an easy time of it. He continued to suffer a great deal with poor health which, he says, stirred him up to 'speak to sinners with some compassion as a dying man to dying men'. He also experienced an intense spiritual struggle. He was assailed by doubts about the fundamental principles of Christianity. However, this made him re-examine the foundations of his faith and as a result he became more convinced of their truth than ever. He believed that biblical Christianity not only made more sense than any other religion or philosophy, but also it alone had the power to produce real holiness of life. Was it not his personal experience that God's Word and Spirit had worked powerfully in his own life?

Baxter also experienced opposition from some of the local people. On the annual 'Show' (Carnival) Day, there was a parade of painted 'giants' and similar displays passing through the streets. On those days some of the more vicious sort would come and 'vent their spleen' against him as part of their amusement. At another time, one of the local drunks saw Baxter sheltering under a tree during a thunderstorm while a well-known woman of illrepute sheltered on the other side. He decided he would make this into an interesting tale to tell amongst his fellow drunks. The slander spread like wildfire and was only checked when the drunk who invented it confessed in a magistrate's court. Another incident followed Baxter's preaching of a sermon on original sin. Some misunderstood him to have said that God hates infants and when this was passed around, it produced much ill feeling towards Baxter. However, he was able to clear away this misconception in his sermon the following Sunday. A more serious incident occurred when the churchwarden was dismantling a crucifix in the churchyard following a directive from Parliament for the removal of images from church property. A gang of local ruffians was passing by and, when they saw what was happening, became infuriated against Baxter. Thankfully, he had gone out for about an hour. However, they came across two of his friends and beat them so badly they later died. Baxter was deeply shocked by this tragedy and by the general prejudice aroused against him. In his next sermon he said he would leave Kidderminster rather than cause them to be guilty of his murder! The people, by that time, had also come to regret this incident and begged him to stay.

During 1642 the quarrel between King Charles I and Parliament rapidly deteriorated into civil war. Most godly men, or 'Puritans', were drawn to the Parliament side, whilst the more profane were drawn to the King's side. Worcestershire was a staunchly Royalist county, and those who were suspected of siding with Parliament were dealt with roughly. It thus became unsafe for Baxter to remain in Kidderminster. Whilst the King's declarations were being read in the marketplace, the reader, a local man, seeing Baxter passing by, stopped and shouted, 'There goeth a traitor!' Following this incident Baxter took his friends' advice and moved to Gloucester for his safety. After spending a month there, he was persuaded to return to Kidderminster, but he found the 'drunken rabble greatly stirred up by their royalist masters'. In the meantime, the King raised an army at Shrewsbury and then headed for

Oxford. They passed close by Kidderminster and a scouting party was seen on nearby Kinver Edge. Some Parliamentarian troops in Kidderminster, believing the rest of the army was coming their way, fled so rapidly they left some carriages and supplies in the town square. At the same time, the main Parliament army, commanded by the Earl of Essex, marched towards Worcester. Conflict was now inevitable. Baxter was preaching in Alcester one Sunday in September 1642 when the sound of distant canon fire was heard. Reports from the battlefront were confusing, so Baxter went to Edgehill to see for himself. He found the two opposing armies facing each other across a battlefield littered with corpses from the recent encounter. However, there was no further fighting and the two armies drew off. Baxter now felt that Kidderminster was far too unsafe so he went instead to Coventry which was a Parliamentary stronghold.

Baxter stayed in Coventry for two years in relative peace and security. He was able to find time for study and he preached regularly to the soldiers and the local people. In the meantime, the tide of the war was turning against the Royalists. Oliver Cromwell was rising in prestige and influence with every victory won by his invincible regiment, nicknamed the 'Ironsides'. Following the battle of Naseby in 1645, Baxter was concerned about the safety of some friends who were serving with the Parliamentarian army. So he went to their field headquarters near Leicester and was relieved to find his friends were well. However, he was alarmed to find the army was being infiltrated by those he considered religious extremists. He was especially concerned about the prevalence of Antinomian[1] teachings amongst the soldiers. The aim

1. The Antinomians believed that the Ten Commandments were irrelevant for Christians who should be guided by the 'law of the Spirit' instead. Although those who preached this error were not necessarily immoral themselves, this was always the danger. Those

of the war had also changed from countering the threat of
Roman Catholicism[2] and the excessive power of Charles I.
It was now being directed more against the monarchy itself
and the power of the bishops. Baxter felt that Cromwell was
encouraging these changes. He now regretted his decision to
decline an invitation from Cromwell to be his chaplain two
years previously. This would have given him the opportunity
to be a restraining influence on the extremists. Consequently,
when he received, from Colonel Whalley, another invitation
to become a regimental chaplain, after consulting some fellow
ministers, Baxter accepted. However, the soldiers of Coventry
were very reluctant to let him go and threatened to bar the
gates to prevent him leaving. To persuade them, Baxter felt
he had to tell them about his concerns for the army and
the reasons for going. Amongst the crowd was a friend of
Cromwell's, and so, when Baxter arrived at the camp, he was
seen as a Royalist sympathiser. He therefore received a rather
cool reception from Oliver Cromwell and was never invited
to join the army council meetings.

Baxter saw action with Colonel Whalley's regiment in the
West Country, including the sieges of Bridgwater and Bristol.
During the siege of Bristol he was taken ill with the plague and

belonging to the sect called the Ranters actually did slide into
blasphemy and immorality. They took Antinomian teaching to its
logical conclusion and taught that our outward actions do not matter.
What mattered was listening to 'Christ' within. The Quakers held
similar beliefs, except they went to the opposite end of the external
morality spectrum into asceticism.

2. One of the factors that had triggered off the Civil War had been the
terrible massacre of 200,000 Protestants during a Roman Catholic
uprising in Ireland in 1641. People were fearful that something similar
was being planned for England. It was well known that the sympathies
of Charles I leant in the direction of Catholicism and there were many
other sympathisers in positions of influence in the country. The Jesuits
were strongly suspected of being behind many plots to bring the
English Church back under the domination of Rome.

128

again feared for his life. However, he recovered, and following the siege of Worcester had the great joy of being able to go and see his friends at Kidderminster again. The war now being effectively over, they expected Baxter to return to them. However, he felt his moderating influence in the army was needed more than ever. But, early in 1647, illness struck again whilst he was with the army near Ashby-de-la-Zouch. After losing several pints of blood due to a nasal haemorrhage, he was much too weak to continue. Lady Rous, of Rous Lench, Worcestershire, a godly woman and a supporter of Baxter, hearing of his illness, sent for him and nursed him back to health. It was at this time, when he was near to death, that he began writing his best-known book *The Saints' Everlasting Rest*. After three months he had written most of this work and was well enough to return to Kidderminster.

Richard Baxter, the most outstanding pastor, Evangelist and writer on practical and devotional themes that Puritanism produced.

Dr J. I. Packer

Chapter 4. Return to Kidderminster

When Richard Baxter returned to Kidderminster in 1647 he found the Civil War had brought some changes that were helpful to his ministry. For one thing, many of those who had opposed him had joined the Royalist army and had been killed in action. Also, the government at this time actively encouraged gospel preaching, in contrast to the government of Charles I. During these times, godliness was no longer despised, but regarded by most people as honourable and praiseworthy. In fact, in the gracious providence of God, the conditions were just right for the events that were about to take place.

At this time Baxter was at the peak of his preaching abilities. In his preaching he sought to make the Bible relevant to the spiritual needs of the people and was aimed primarily at the understanding and conscience of his hearers. His style of preaching is clearly seen in his books such as *A Call to the Unconverted* and *The Saint's Everlasting Rest* which were prepared from sermonic material. His method was to use argument upon argument to reason with and to persuade the people of their need to repent and to believe in Christ. A friend of Baxter said, 'In his sermons there was a rare union of arguments and motives to convince the mind and gain the heart; all the fountains of reason and persuasion were open to his discerning eye.'[1]

The main thrust of his ministry was evangelistic. He said, 'The work of conversion is the first thing we must drive at and labour with all our might to effect; then to build up those that are truly converted.' He felt an almost overwhelming compassion for the souls of the lost, and he strongly resisted the temptation to provide a display of fine oratory for those who came in search of novelty or entertainment. He mainly preached the great fundamental truths of the Christian faith. However, he always included something above the understanding of his hearers to prevent them becoming complacent or conceited and to stimulate their desire to learn more. He was not the sort of evangelist who would have been content with a mere shallow 'decision for Christ'. Baxter was concerned that the work of conversion should be thorough. As a result, the faith of those converted under his ministry withstood the tests of both severe persecution and time.

His preaching not only appealed to the mind, but also moved the heart. Baxter preached with great urgency and seriousness as he pleaded with sinners to 'embrace the Redeemer with a lively faith'. Towards the close of *A Call to the Unconverted* you can well imagine tears rolling down his cheeks as he pleads with his hearers, 'If I came hungry or naked to one of your doors, would you not part with more than a cup of water to relieve me? I am confident you would: if it were to save my life I know you would, some of you, hazard your own. And yet will not be entreated to

---

1.   Dr William Bates.

part with your sensual pleasures for your own salvation?' This style of preaching contrasted greatly with that of the average clergyman of the day who usually discoursed drowsily on the virtues of doing good. Baxter movingly brought his people face to face with the great realities of heaven and of hell, with God and with eternity. His prayers were also full of life and feeling. It was said that 'when he prayed his soul took wing for heaven and wrapt up the souls of others with him'. Yet despite all this he often reproached himself for not being fervent enough.

Such preaching, far from deterring the people, attracted them in such large numbers that the parish church, which held about one thousand, was filled beyond its capacity so that five galleries had to be erected to accommodate the greatly enlarged congregation. The main occupation of the people of Kidderminster in those days was weaving, so there were few rich people amongst them. Baxter observed the truth of our Lord's teaching that it is hard for the rich to enter the kingdom of heaven, but the poor received the gospel gladly. The most serious opposition to his work came from the wealthy and respectable Sir Ralph Clare. Although he always treated Baxter with the utmost politeness and civility, he nevertheless refused to embrace the gospel himself and kept his family and servants away from the meetings. Because he was well respected, others followed his bad example. However, there were some wealthy and influential people who were enthusiastic supporters of Baxter including many local J.P.s. Another advantage was that the people were able to read good books or talk about spiritual matters whilst working at their looms. The people had never heard preaching like this before, and so they embraced the teaching before they had time to become 'gospel-hardened' as had happened to the people of Bridgnorth.

The message of Baxter's preaching was reinforced by his personal work. Every week, on Mondays and Tuesdays, he and his assistant would, between them, visit fourteen families to instruct them systematically (catechise) in the fundamental teachings of Scripture. Their aim was to visit every one of the eight hundred or so families in the parish every year. 'Another great help to my success', he writes, 'was the work of personal conference with every family apart, with catechising and instructing them'. He was horrified to discover that many who seemed to have listened carefully to his preaching did not even know the basic teachings of Christianity. By teaching them individually they were able to learn more in half an hour than they had from hundreds of sermons.

He also provided a great deal of material assistance to the poor and needy. His annual income was £80 to £90 plus £60 to £80 a year from the sale of his books. Most of this he gave away. He paid for the education of children from the families who could not afford it, and the ablest of the children he sent to university. Some of these had been converted through Baxter's ministry and became preachers themselves. His charity was indiscriminate. 'In giving the little I had', says Baxter, 'I did not enquire whether they were good or bad if they asked for relief; for the bad had souls and bodies that needed charity most'. Realising the great value of reading good books, he gave his writings to his people. He gave a copy of the smaller books to every family. If a family was too poor to afford a Bible he gave them one. He visited the sick and comforted the dying. For some years, the town was without a doctor, and many people turned to Baxter for medical help. Through receiving so many treatments for his own various ailments he had gained some experience that was helpful to others. This was always given free of charge. However, he realised his limitations and, after some time, he arranged for a 'godly, diligent physician' to come and set up a practice in the town. Because he had done so much good among them, the people were all the more ready to listen to his teaching. Amongst his first converts were many young people. When the parents saw the improvement in their children, their prejudices were overcome.

A common problem of the time was drunkenness, and a couple of notorious drunks lived near Baxter. They would regularly rant and rave in the streets, one by day and the other by night. They would often be put in the stocks until they sobered up, but they invariably lapsed again when they were released. There was a young man in the church who lapsed into this sin. He was repeatedly warned by Baxter, and he would relent for a while, but lapsed into his old ways every time. Finally, he was publicly warned and barred from Communion, and the people were advised to have nothing to do with him. This was to 'convince him of his misery and the necessity of true repentance and reformation'. After this he would rail and curse at Baxter's door and would 'prophesy' judgments against Kidderminster in the marketplace. Once he tried to murder Baxter in the churchyard. However, when he grabbed Baxter's cloak it came away, and before he could do any more harm a couple of bystanders restrained him and took him to the magistrates. 'And thus he continued', wrote Baxter, 'raging against me about a year, and then died of a fever in horror of conscience'. The outrageous behaviour of these men served as a warning to many people against this particular vice.

Baxter only preached once on a Sunday.[2] On Thursday evenings he held a meeting in his own home during which

---

2. Before the Civil War, he had usually preached twice on a Sunday.

the previous Sunday's sermon was reviewed by question and answer. The people then had an opportunity to raise any doubts or difficulties they may have had about the sermon or spiritual problems, and Baxter would try to answer their difficulties and resolve their doubts. He would then ask two or three of them to pray and the meeting was closed with the singing of a psalm. Those who were too shy or too inexperienced to pray on those occasions would meet together on a Saturday night to read, to pray and to prepare themselves for the following Sabbath day. The younger believers learned how to pray by following the example of their elders.

Thus Baxter laboured solidly for fourteen years in Kidderminster, and the Lord was pleased to bless the ministry of his servant to an extraordinary degree. Apart from the meetings being packed out as already mentioned, he says that, 'On the Lord's-days there was no disorder to be seen in the streets, but you might hear a hundred families singing psalms and repeating sermons as you passed through the streets. In a word, when I came thither first there was about one family in a street that worshipped God and called on his name, and when I came away there was not passed one family in the side of a street that did not so, and that did not, by professing serious godliness, give us hopes of their sincerity. And those families which were the worst, being inns and alehouses, usually some persons in each house did seem to be religious'. Of the six hundred or so communicants, Baxter said he had good hopes for the sincerity of the faith of all but twelve of them. When news of the wonderful change in Kidderminster spread, it won the approval of Anabaptists and Independents who hardly

However, due to his poor health, he was unable to speak for more than an hour without, as he says, 'the prostration of my strength and extream languishing of my body'. The evening services were usually taken by Richard Sargeant, the new curate.

believed it possible that God could work through the ministry of a parish church. Indeed, one of the blessings Baxter thanks God for was the unity amongst his people. They were not torn by the strife and dissension produced by sectarianism seen in so many other places at that time.

However, during all that time he records that he was seldom free from pain. Many times he was brought low and felt near to death. At such times his friends would gather around and pray for him. The Lord heard their prayers and restored him. On one occasion he says he was ill for three weeks, until his friends prayed for him and he recovered that very day. That was a Good Friday and following his recovery he felt able to resume his pastoral responsibilities. Until this time he had felt unable to administer the Lord's Supper to those about whose faith he was unsure. Now, because there had been such a clear work of God in the lives of so many, he no doubt felt it was time to change. So, after preaching, he administered the sacraments to the flock. Having done so he says, 'I was much revived and eased of my infirmities'. This experience, he says, was repeated on every subsequent occasion when he preached and administered Holy Communion. Apart from his illnesses, Baxter records his thankfulness to God for preserving him in several accidents. At one time, whilst working in his study, the top shelf broke and showered down some very weighty volumes which landed either side of him.

During these years in Kidderminster, amongst all his other labours, Baxter found time to write sixty books.[3] Among them were some of his best-known works, *The Saints' Everlasting Rest*, *A Call to the Unconverted* and *The Reformed Pastor*. In all

---

3. Richard Baxter was the most prolific writer of his time. It has been calculated that his total literary output would be equivalent to sixty octavo volumes, or some thirty to forty thousand closely printed pages.

his labours, Baxter regarded preaching and sermon preparation as recreational activities! He had no spare time for anything else, and regretted he had so very little time for his studies. It is little wonder that he considered being single as an advantage at this time. Being free from family responsibilities, he came to regard his flock as his children and lavished his love and care upon them instead.

Although his work in Kidderminster took up so much of his time and energy, Baxter's vision extended beyond the confines of his parish. He regularly preached in the surrounding area in places such as Cleobury, Shifnal and Dudley. In Dudley, the place of his first ministry, his preaching was so popular that the people not only filled the church, but also hung on the windows and ledges to hear him. Moreover, it was his heart's desire that the cause of the gospel would flourish throughout the whole country and even beyond. Many of his books were translated into foreign languages and were avidly read by Christians on the continent. Richard Baxter had a great burden for foreign missionary work. 'There is nothing in the world that lieth so heavily upon my heart', he wrote, 'as the thought of the miserable nations of the earth. It is the most astonishing part of all God's providence to me, that he so far forsaketh almost all the world, and confineth his special favour to so few; that so small a part of the world hath the profession of Christianity'. It is, therefore, hardly surprising to find that Baxter was an active supporter of John Eliot, the 'apostle' to the American Indians. Following his translation of the Bible into the Algonquian language, the next book Eliot translated was Baxter's *A Call to the Unconverted*. Baxter was a leading figure in the movement for the establishment of the first missionary organisation, the Society for the Propagation of the Gospel (1701).

Chapter 5. The Restoration

The anti-Royalist sentiments Richard Baxter had witnessed amongst Oliver Cromwell's supporters in the army culminated in the trial and execution of Charles I on 30 January 1649. His son and heir, Charles II, managed to win the support of the Scots by convincing them that he was a true Protestant and that he favoured the Presbyterian form of church government. During this 'Commonwealth'[1] period great liberty was allowed to all religious groups as long as they were basically Protestant. The Scots made an agreement with Charles II. They would provide him with an army to set him on the throne in return for his establishment of a Presbyterian form of church government throughout the realm. However, this plan came to grief following the Battle of Worcester, on 30 September 1651. Cromwell's troops routed the Scots who fled north and many went through Kidderminster. A detachment of Cromwell's troops guarding the bridge at nearby Bewdley came to Kidderminster to cut off their retreat. They took up position in the square, and in the ensuing skirmish, bullets struck Baxter's door and windows until midnight when the fighting stopped. Charles himself escaped, passing through the outskirts of Kidderminster, and spent that night hiding in an oak tree in Boscobel on the Shropshire and Staffordshire

1. The 'Commonwealth' period was the name given to the period between the overthrow of Charles I and the restoration of Charles II. The country was governed by various Parliaments and finally by Cromwell when he became 'Protector' in December 1652.

border. From there he fled to France, escaping detection by dressing up as a servant.

As we have witnessed recently in some Eastern European countries, the overthrow of a ruthless, totalitarian regime does not necessarily result in peace and harmony. Those who had fought together for the overthrow of Charles I now quarrelled amongst themselves. They had won the war, but they lost the peace. The political turbulence that followed the Civil War was only brought under control by Cromwell's benevolent dictatorship. There were controversies about various forms of church government and many sects flourished at this time of religious toleration.[2] Many people became weary of the various attempts to find a satisfactory form of government and they came to believe the return of the monarchy was the best solution. Indeed, many Englishmen, even those on the side of Parliament, like Baxter, had never wanted to abolish the monarchy altogether. They had only wanted to reduce the political power of Charles I and prevent him being manipulated by those who wanted England to return to Roman Catholicism. Baxter, during the one time he preached before Oliver Cromwell, had criticised him for weakening the church by encouraging divisions. The Protector was not too pleased by this and later summoned Baxter to a private audience during which he lectured Baxter for an hour. Baxter replied by asking Cromwell why he had abolished the monarchy at which Cromwell became quite angry. A few days later Cromwell again summoned Baxter to discuss liberty of conscience in the presence of most of the Privy Council. Cromwell again lectured him 'tediously' and seemed to pay little attention to Baxter's views.

---

2.   Sects such as the Quakers, and others with such descriptive names as the Ranters, the Seekers, the Levellers and the Fifth Monarchists.

When Oliver Cromwell died in September 1658, his son Richard succeeded him as Protector. However, Richard Cromwell did not have his father's leadership abilities and resigned in April 1659. The Royalists and Presbyterians then formed an alliance and there followed a power struggle with the 'Republicans' who opposed the restoration of the King. In February 1660, the Royalist party won when General Monk, at the head of the northern army, intervened to take control of the situation in London. On 4 April Charles II issued a declaration containing promises designed to make his restoration seem almost irresistible to Parliament.[3] One of his promises was that he would ensure liberty of conscience to various religious groups. The situation was now rapidly approaching a critical point. Therefore, on 13 April Baxter decided it was his duty to go to London and throw the weight of his influence behind moves for the restoration of Charles II. Parliament called for a day of prayer and fasting and requested Dr Calamy,[4] Dr Gauden[5] and Richard Baxter to preach and to pray with them. This was the day before they voted in favour of formally calling for the return of Charles II. At that time the Lord Mayor and aldermen of the City of London decided to hold a Day of Solemn Thanksgiving to God for General Monk's success, and they requested Baxter to preach in St Paul's.

Charles II returned to England on 25 May 1660 amidst the general rejoicing of the people. As a favour to the Presbyterians

---

3. The Declaration of Breda.
4. Edmund Calamy (1600–1666), a Presbyterian leader. Not to be confused with his grandson of the same name (1671–1732) who wrote an abridgement of Richard Baxter's autobiography and also the History of the Nonconformists.
5. Dr Gauden was another leading Presbyterian who later became a bishop.

and other religious leaders who had helped bring about the restoration, some were made king's chaplains, including Dr Calamy, Dr Manton, Richard Baxter and nine others. A short while afterwards, Dr Manton, Baxter and some others had an audience with Charles. They requested that the advantages for the gospel gained during the previous years should not be lost and that the King should support moves for unity amongst God's people. Charles received their requests with much apparent grace and favour. He expressed his hearty agreement and desire for a compromise between the various church factions, and pledged his active support. One of the elderly ministers in the delegation was so overwhelmed by the King's kind promises that he burst into tears of joy and thanked His Majesty.

After this meeting, Charles requested the Presbyterians[6] to draw up a list of proposals for church unity. The King would not allow them time for a full consultation. They would have to act on their own initiative and consult with those ministers who were in London itself. They met in Sion College and, following some lengthy discussions, drew up their list of proposals for church government and church discipline. During the ensuing negotiations,[7] these proposals were firmly rejected by the Episcopalians[8] who submitted no proposals

6. Richard Baxter was included with the Presbyterians during these negotiations, even though he was not a Presbyterian himself. He did not believe their office of lay elder was scriptural. Baxter was a 'moderate Episcopalian'. However, their positions were so similar in many respects that many considered them practically identical.

7. These took place at the Bishop of London's residence and subsequently became known as the 'Savoy Conference'.

8. The Episcopalians sought to restore church government to exactly the same as it was before the Civil War, with the traditional bishops and archbishops, etc. On the other hand, Richard Baxter and his friends wanted a 'moderate' form of episcopacy in which the bishop was only a first among equals alongside his fellow ministers exercising his rule and authority only with their consent.

of their own and remained inflexible in their position. The bishops were intent on restoring the prestige, the wealth and the power they enjoyed before the Civil War. They saw Baxter, their chief spokesman, and his fellow Puritans as a potential threat, especially when they were unable to match his skill in debate and argument.

During the negotiations, Charles, by means of the Lord Chancellor, offered Baxter the bishopric of Hereford. He refused to give a definite reply until the contents of the Declaration, which the king was due to make, were known.[9] However, Baxter was hesitant to accept this offer for other reasons. He felt it would leave him little time for his writing for one thing. He was also suspicious of King Charles' motives in this matter. He could foresee that, even at best, many godly ministers would not agree with their proposals, and part of a bishop's work would then be to ensure these men were silenced. He did not relish the thought of joining the opposition one bit. Furthermore, he was convinced that the diocesan system of church government[10] was unbiblical. Two of Baxter's fellow negotiators, Edmund Calamy and Dr Reynolds were also offered bishoprics. The aim was, no doubt, to win them over and thereby weaken the Puritan opposition. Reynolds accepted and became Bishop of Norwich, whereas Baxter and Calamy refused.

When the King's Declarations were finally published, Baxter was pleasantly surprised to find some important concessions had been made to his position. However, he refused to attach too much importance to these since they could be withdrawn at any time unless they were passed into law. Despite many pleas, this never happened. During one of the meetings

9. This became known as the Worcester House Declaration.
10. The hierarchical form of church government by bishops and archbishops.

for negotiation, King Charles introduced a proposal that had been submitted by the Independents and Anabaptists calling for freedom of worship. Charles, no doubt, hoped that its acceptance would also allow Roman Catholicism to be reintroduced into England. No one dared answer this proposal until Baxter suggested that Roman Catholics and Socinians[11] be exempted from this liberty. This suggestion displeased Charles who then promptly adjourned the meeting.

At this time, Richard Baxter requested the favour of being restored to his flock in Kidderminster. He had officially lost his pastorate as part of the restoration agreement with King Charles in which positions and property sequestered during the Commonwealth were restored. The vicar of Kidderminster[12] was under the influence of Sir Ralph Clare and refused to allow Baxter to return under any circumstances, even though he had offered to preach for nothing. After preaching on two or three occasions to the people of Kidderminster, the vicar banned him from preaching any more. Baxter requested the opportunity to preach a farewell sermon and administer Communion to his former flock, but this too was denied. Finally, he left a godly man, Mr Baldwin, to minister in his stead. Whilst Baxter was visiting his sick father in Shropshire, Mr Baldwin came to him with the news that he too had been forbidden to preach. As a last resort, Baxter decided to seek permission from the bishop of Worcester to return to Kidderminster, even though he knew the bishop was no

---

11. Those who followed the teaching of Socinius who maintained that the death of Christ was only a good example of faith and obedience for Christians to follow.

12. Mr Danse had continued to live in the vicarage and received some income during the time Baxter was in Kidderminster. Richard Baxter had refused the offer to replace Mr Danse, but the citizens had secretly organised his official appointment as minister without his knowledge.

friend of the gospel, and many friends entreated him not to go fearing his arrest.[13] However, Baxter did see the bishop, and, although he was not arrested, the bishop forbade him to preach in his diocese. Baxter was deeply saddened by this failure to return to Kidderminster. 'Having parted with my dear flock', he says, 'I need not say without mutual sense and tears, I left Mr Baldwin[14] to live privately among them and oversee them in my stead, and visit them from home to home; advising them, notwithstanding all the injuries they had received and all the failings of the ministers that preached to them and the defects of the present way of worship, that yet they should keep to the public assemblies and make use of such helps as might be had in public, together with this private help ...' (i.e. Mr Baldwin's ministry).

Following this unsuccessful attempt to return to Kidderminster, Baxter spent the rest of his life in and around London. He preached in various churches in the city for a year. He then joined Dr Bates in St Dunstan's-in-the-West in Fleet Street where he preached once a week to crowded congregations. Whilst preaching there on one occasion, an incident occurred that demonstrates something of Baxter's courage and composure. In the middle of the sermon some bricks and plaster fell from the roof of the steeple. Nobody

---

13. It was even rumoured that a Worcestershire knight had placed his soldiers at the bishop's disposal for the express purpose of arresting Richard Baxter.
14. Mr Baldwin was curate of Chaddesley, about four miles from Kidderminster, until he was ejected with the other Nonconformists in 1662. He continued to pastor Richard Baxter's 'flock', who continued to gather for worship in the outbuildings of a house in Mill Street. They later constituted themselves into a Congregational Church. Baxter described Mr Baldwin as a 'good scholar ... and an extraordinary preacher'. He died in January 1693, six months before the opening of their own meeting house.

was hurt, but the congregation panicked and stampeded for the exit. The noise of the running feet of many people in the galleries also resembled the sound of falling masonry, which added to the panic. Richard Baxter stayed in the pulpit, and when he could be heard, he calmed the crowd and continued preaching. Only a few moments later, a pew gave way under the weight of so many people sitting on it. The sound of breaking timber made people think the roof was collapsing, and an even worse panic ensued. Baxter again pacified the crowd and eventually finished his sermon without further interruption. During the extensive repair works on the building following this incident, Baxter preached in St Bride's at the other end of Fleet Street. He also preached at Blackfriars on Sundays and a midweek lecture in Milk Street. Baxter continued preaching in these churches for about a year until 1662, when he was forbidden by law from any further public ministry.

At this time, Baxter rapidly fell from the favour he had recently enjoyed and was slandered in 'court, city and country'. During 1661, a new Parliament was called, which was distinctly cavalier in character. With the bishops also back in the House of Lords, the political tide had now turned very markedly against the Puritans. Both Parliament and the bishops were intent on ensuring they would never again suffer humiliation at the hands of the Puritans as they had during the Civil War and its aftermath. If the Puritans refused to compromise they would be ruthlessly suppressed. There followed a number of very unjust laws passed against them. One of these was the Corporation Act, which restricted the holding of any public office to Anglicans. The other was the notorious Act of Uniformity, which required clergy to subscribe, amongst other things, to a new prayer book which the bishops had deliberately made offensive to the

Puritans. The deadline for their acceptance of this Act was Bartholomew's Day, 24 August 1662, when two thousand of the most godly pastors in the land refused to subscribe and were consequently ejected from their ministries. This event reminded many of the Bartholomew's Day ninety years previously when three thousand French Protestants were massacred in Paris. Baxter had already made his position clear when he stopped preaching the previous May soon after the Act had received royal assent. He did so partly so that those who looked to him for a lead would have no doubts about his position. Many of these ejected ministers faced serious hardships from poverty and persecution. Some continued to preach in the open air, in streets or in the fields. Some were imprisoned or banished when they refused to be silenced.[15] Many fled overseas, some to the American colonies, and Baxter was tempted to join them. However, he decided to stay in England when he considered that in his poor state of health he probably would not have survived the hardship of a long sea voyage in those days.

---

15. A notable example was John Bunyan the Baptist preacher. It was whilst he was in prison in Bedford for refusing to stop preaching that he wrote his famous *Pilgrim's Progress.*

Chapter 6. Marriage

It was during these very difficult times for Richard Baxter that the Lord graciously provided a 'help meet' for him. Margaret Charlton was the daughter of Francis and Mary Charlton of Apley Castle, near Wellington, Shropshire, just over three miles from Baxter's own birthplace. Her father had died when she was a young girl, and her mother remarried a Mr Hanmer who was a staunch Royalist. When she was a girl of eight, she witnessed the horrors of war when Apley Castle was stormed and partially burned down by Parliamentarian troops. Her mother was a true believer in Christ, and after she was widowed for the second time, she came to live in Kidderminster in 1658. Margaret, who had been living with her married sister in Oxford, soon came to join her mother. At first she disliked the godliness and simplicity of life in Kidderminster. She loved to dress in expensive, eye-catching clothes and enjoyed reading romantic novels. However, it was not long before the gospel preached by Baxter began to change her life. His teaching was 'received on her heart as the seal on the wax', and she surrendered her life to the claims of the Lord Jesus Christ.

Margaret's conversion was both sudden and dramatic, and was a cause for great joy and encouragement to the Christians of Kidderminster. The change in her life was clear for all to see. Instead of reading novels she could often be overheard praying fervently in her private room. However, in the winter of 1659 she became very ill and near to death. Baxter arranged a day of special prayer and fasting for her on New Year's Eve 1659. There was an almost miraculous answer to their prayers, and Margaret was well enough to attend a special service of thanksgiving on 10 April 1660.

There are some indications that it was about this time that she began to fall in love with Richard Baxter. She struggled against her feelings and tried unsuccessfully to overcome them. It was well known that Baxter considered it advantageous for a pastor to remain single to give himself fully to the work of the ministry. It is possible he suspected Margaret's love for him was more than admiration or normal affection. In one letter he counsels her against excessive 'creature love'. Anyway, there is no hint that he gave her any encouragement at all. On the contrary, he seems to have discouraged any notions of romance whatsoever.

Richard Baxter left Kidderminster for London three days after the thanksgiving service for her deliverance on 10 April. In one of his letters, he told Margaret and her mother not to follow him to London. However, they ignored his advice and came anyway. Margaret's mother died in 1661, leaving her alone and in need of a protector. As we have already noted, Baxter's preaching ministry ended on 25 May 1662. There was then no longer any reason why he should not marry. It is not clear when Baxter began to feel a special affection for Margaret. Late in 1661, a rumour had been spread about, by Bishop Morley, 'with all the odium he could put upon it' that Baxter was already married. This rumour may have been based on someone having witnessed signs of a growing affection between Richard and Margaret, but we cannot be sure. However, we do know they were married on 10 September 1662 by Mr Samuel Clark. Baxter later referred to 'many strange occurrences', no doubt recognising the hand of Providence in bringing them together. Baxter recorded no details because he goes on to say, 'Wise friends, by whom I am advised, think it better to omit such personal particularities, at least at this time'. His friends probably did not want to provide 'fuel' for rumour-mongers. However, we do know that while Margaret was lodging in Aldersgate, Richard was staying with a friend, not far away, in Little Britain.

Richard Baxter was twenty-four years older than Margaret, and although they had no children, they were very happily married for nineteen years. Soon after their marriage, Margaret's depression, which she had suffered for some time, immediately lifted. He says this was partly due to counsel and partly because she was happily occupied with domestic duties. Baxter stipulated certain conditions to their marriage. One of these was that he would not benefit from anything that belonged to his wife before their marriage. Margaret came from a wealthy family, and Richard was eager to allay any suspicion that he had married for money. Another condition was that Margaret would allow her husband to give priority to his ministerial work. Margaret proved to be an excellent wife and companion for Richard. She was very practical, and a woman of great wit and wisdom. She had inherited a substantial sum of money from her parents' estates and devoted herself to works of charity. She was especially concerned for those who were imprisoned for debt, particularly those who were the 'most worthy'.[1] Margaret denied herself, dressing in modest clothes and eating plain food, to be able to give more help to others.

Margaret Baxter was also well educated and had a better knowledge of Latin, Greek and Hebrew than her husband.

---

1. Although Baxter does not say so, this probably refers to Dissenters who were suffering fines and imprisonment for their faith.

Baxter often consulted her in cases of pastoral concern. 'Except in cases that require learning and skill', says Baxter, 'she was better at resolving a case of conscience than most divines that I ever knew in all my life'. Baxter's tender devotion to his wife gives the lie to the caricature of the Puritans as being cold, unemotional and joyless. 'It is my judgement and constant practice', writes Baxter, 'to make those that I teach understand that the gospel is glad tidings of great joy, and that holiness lies especially in delighting in God, his Word, and works and in his joyful praise, and hopes of glory'.

Margaret Baxter was a godly woman who was completely at one with her husband in the cause of the gospel. She strongly encouraged her husband and other preachers of the gospel in their evangelistic enterprises. She was also deeply concerned for the spiritual needs of her relatives and household servants. It upset her if any servants left her employment unconverted. She treated those servants who were converted like her own children. She shared her husband's estimation of the value of good books and gave hundreds away. Margaret was in complete agreement with her husband's refusal to accept the bribe of a bishopric. Later on, in 1669, when Baxter was sent to prison for his faith, Margaret went with him, bringing her 'best bed' with her! 'I think', wrote Baxter, 'that she had scarce a pleasanter time in her life than while she was with me there'. However, she had little patience with those non-conforming ministers who continually moaned and complained about their losses and dangers, and, 'would have no man be a minister that had not so much self denial as to lay down all at the feet of Christ, and count no cost of suffering too dear to serve Him'.

Christ leads me through no darker rooms
Than He went through before;
And he that to God's kingdom comes
Must enter by this door.

Richard Baxter

Chapter 7. The Darkness Gathers

Following the ejection of Richard Baxter along with two thousand or so of his fellow pastors in 1662, these Nonconforming ministers were persecuted ruthlessly by the authorities. They were forbidden to preach or even to meet together for prayer. Their enemies called every gathering a 'dangerous meeting for sedition'. Baxter and his friend, Dr. William Bates, narrowly escaped arrest when they were due to meet to pray for the recovery of a woman who was ill and on the point of death. For various reasons they were unable to attend this meeting, and so all the arresting officers could do was to take the names of those present. However, many godly ministers were fined and imprisoned at this time. The Quakers were also persecuted. Indeed they seemed to invite persecution by preaching openly in public places. For a while they made so much work for the bailiffs that they had little time to harass the Nonconformists. During this time, Baxter preached and prayed with those Presbyterians or Independents who invited him.

In July 1663, Baxter left London because of his health and went to live in Acton, which was then a village six miles west of the capital. In Acton he held meetings in his home for the local people. On one occasion, during a Sunday gathering in 1665, a bullet came through their window and narrowly missed both Baxter and his sister-in-law.

At this time a series of calamities fell on England. Richard Baxter saw these as God's judgments on the nation because of its persecution of God's people. The first calamity was a disastrous trade war with Holland. Then there was a long drought that produced a very poor harvest. This was followed by the Plague during which 100,000 people died in London alone. Baxter thanked God that his family were preserved safely in Acton even though he said the local churchyard resembled a ploughed field because of the large numbers of newly dug graves. During the Plague, the rich people and most of the ministers who had remained in the established church fled from London. The Nonconforming pastors took pity on the poor people left behind and ministered to them in their distress.

Even whilst the Plague was raging, the King and Parliament, who had fled to Oxford to escape, were drawing up new legislation to persecute the Nonconformists. This was the Act of Confinement that forbade Dissenters[1] coming within five miles of a city or town or the place where they had formerly ministered. Some dissenting ministers left for the country, some had to leave their families, some went into hiding, but others were emboldened to preach more openly, until they were arrested and put into prison.

Just after midnight, 2 September 1666, the Great Fire of London started. The weather had been dry for some time and,

---

1. The Nonconformists were also called Dissenters because they dissented from the official practices of the established church.

fanned by an easterly wind, the fire spread rapidly. Within three days, it had engulfed most of the city. From his home in Acton, Baxter saw the flames and a huge pall of smoke that turned the sun red. He saw this as an illustration of the vanity of this life as both rich and poor alike had to stand by helplessly as they watched their houses and all their worldly goods going up in flames. Baxter was also saddened by the loss of thousands of precious books in the fire, which he believed was a great loss to 'piety and learning'. The charred remains of many books fell near his home and even as far away as Windsor.

As if all this was not enough, in June 1667 England suffered a humiliating defeat at the hands of the Dutch. Meeting little resistance, they sailed up the Thames and destroyed some of the most powerful fighting ships of the Royal Navy moored at Chatham docks and towed away some others. It could have been much worse because London itself lay defenceless before them, and they could have wreaked havoc in the capital. Following this calamity, there was a widespread feeling of discontent in the country. People murmured that such things would never have happened in Cromwell's day, however they kept their complaints a secret for fear of the authorities. Also, following poor harvests, the Plague and the Great Fire, there was a general recession of trade and widespread economic hardship. The ministers whom the bishops had placed instead of those ejected were very poor in terms of spiritual quality and ministerial ability. This also produced popular discontent against the bishops.

However, at this time there was some easing of the restrictions against the Nonconformists. Except for a few fanatics, there was little desire to enforce the laws directed against them. Persecution had also brought many of the dissenting groups together in a greater unity than they had experienced before the troubles began. The Nonconformists were therefore greatly encouraged and enjoyed much popular support at this time. One of his wealthy neighbours complained to the King about the large numbers of people who came to the meetings held in Baxter's home in Acton. However, the King did nothing about it. Another influential neighbour of Baxter's was Sir Matthew Hale, Lord Chief Baron of the Exchequer and a man of great ability, godliness and learning. He and Baxter became good friends and he encouraged Baxter's practice of holding meetings for worship in his home.

This, however, only proved to be a brief respite in the persecutions. In 1669, Baxter was arrested for the 'illegal' worship meetings held in his home. Because he refused to promise not to preach the following Sunday, he was sent to Clerkenwell Prison. This unpleasant experience was alleviated by the company of his wife, who also brought with her so many domestic items that he said it was almost as comfortable as being at home! But his persecutors were frustrated when they had to release him a week later, partly due to a technical fault in the arrest warrant and partly due to the influence of his friend, Sir Matthew Hale. Nevertheless, Baxter had to move from Acton, otherwise his persecutors would merely have had to correct the warrant and re-arrest him. So, the Baxters moved to Totteridge near Barnet to a house with 'small and rather smoky rooms', which did not agree with his health.

In 1670, Baxter's book, *The Cure of Church Divisions,* was published, in which he argued that it was good for Christians to continue worshipping in parish churches despite the bitter hostility against Nonconformists. Understandably, many of his old flock in Kidderminster criticised him for this. Following his ejection from Kidderminster, the bishop, the deans and many of the curates had preached long and bitter sermons against Baxter to alienate the people from him. However, the people had become alienated against the bishops and clergy instead. They began to meet in private houses where they read sermons and prayed together. For this 'crime', many of them were fined or had their goods confiscated, and others were imprisoned. Yet, despite all this, Baxter wrote, 'not one that I hear of are fallen off or forsake their uprightness'. But now, the Kidderminster Christians felt their former pastor was failing to give them the kind of support they expected from him.

The book just mentioned also gave rise to a rumour that Baxter was about to conform. As a result, the Earl of Lauderdale, a friend and admirer of Baxter's, with the King's permission, offered him any position he desired in Scotland, either a church, a bishopric or a university position. Baxter, for reasons of conscience, declined the offer. If anything, the persecution in Scotland was even worse than it was in England. At that time hundreds of Scotish Covenanters[2] were brutally martyred for their faith in Christ. One wonders why Baxter felt so attached to the established Church after all that he, as well as the majority of true believers in the land, had suffered at its hands. It may be that he still clung to his vision of a united national Church. He had always laboured for unity amongst believers. He felt that, following the restoration of Charles II, a great opportunity had been lost to turn England into a 'land of saints' through the preaching of the gospel. He hoped the wonderful changes in Kidderminster could have been repeated in every parish in the land. He felt the blame for this lay with the sects on one hand and the bishops on the other.

---

2. Those who signed the 'National League and Covenant' to acknowledge no other head of the Church than Jesus Christ.

In 1672, King Charles II issued a 'Declaration of Indulgence' granting religious freedom. His real purpose was to further the cause of Roman Catholicism.[3] However, this also gave some 'breathing space' to the Nonconformists. Baxter, along with many other dissenting preachers, was now able to obtain a licence to preach legally once more. In January 1673, he began a regular Friday lecture in a church near Fetter Lane. In Easter that year, the Baxters moved to a house in Bloomsbury. This liberty was short-lived, however. Parliament, deeply suspicious of the King's intentions, proclaimed his Declaration illegal in February. Some magistrates renewed their persecution of the Nonconformists, but most were reluctant to do so.

In July 1674, Richard Baxter was preaching in St James's Market House when the main beam, supporting the floor, creaked several times under the weight of the people who had crowded in to hear him. Remembering the earlier incident in St Dunstan's, Baxter, with a calm authority, pacified the people and continued preaching. However, the following day, when the floorboards were removed, the main beam was found to be so deeply cracked in two places they ascribed the fact that it had not given way to a 'wonder of [God's] providence'. These meetings were attended with great blessing. Baxter had preached to large congregations who listened very attentively. Many of them showed, by their marked change of life, that they had been truly converted. Many, including former Roman Catholics, gave public thanks to God for their conversion.

---

3. Charles was an admirer of Louis XIV of France who was ruthlessly persecuting the Huguenot (Protestant) Christians in his own country at that time. Charles and Louis signed a treaty in which Louis would give financial aid to Charles in return for military help against the Netherlands and on condition that Charles would embrace the Roman Catholic faith, which he secretly did. James, the Duke of York, the King's brother and future King had already declared himself a Roman Catholic.

Lord it belongs not to my care
Whether I die or live;
To love and serve Thee is my share
And this Thy grace must give.

Richard Baxter

Chapter 8. Spies and Informers

Following Parliament's announcement that the King's Declaration of Indulgence was illegal, persecution was renewed when the Nonconformists' licences to preach were recalled. The bishops hired spies and informers to track down dissenting preachers and to bring them to trial. Richard Baxter was among the first to be arrested. The bailiff of Westminster, a Mr Barwell, went around all the city judges for a warrant for Baxter's arrest. However, they all refused to grant him one. Nevertheless, he was able to obtain a warrant from a county judge, Sir John Medlicot, and promptly sent his informer, a Mr Keting, with the warrant to arrest Baxter. Whilst they were waiting to see the magistrate, Baxter spoke kindly to Mr Keting regarding the needs of his soul, which, 'his conscience did not well digest'. On this occasion, Baxter was again released on a technicality because his 'offence' was committed in the city, and only a city judge had the authority to sign a warrant. A few days later, Mr Barwell, the bailiff, died tragically in a riding accident, and soon afterwards, Sir John Medlicot, the judge, also died suddenly. Mr Keting, the informer, had suffered pangs of conscience ever since Baxter had spoken to him, and he was now terrified because of the death of his master. He came to Baxter and begged his forgiveness. However, spies continued to attend Baxter's preaching services to try and gain evidence against him. During one of these services, Baxter preached so powerfully on 'Making light of Christ and his salvation', that two spies in the congregation fled in terror!

Due to the crowds coming to hear Baxter's preaching some of his friends built a large meeting house for him in Oxenden Street, which was completed on 16 April 1676. Seeing the great spiritual needs of the people, Margaret Baxter urged the building of another meeting house in Bloomsbury. However, Baxter had only preached in his new meeting house once when the authorities moved to arrest him once more. At the same time, he suffered a severe bout of his recurring illness, and his friends persuaded him to move to the country for a while for the sake of his health as well as his liberty. At this time he decided to dispose of all but his essential possessions, and hid his library of books (his most treasured possession) with a view to selling them also. Baxter said he was glad to part with all so that he had nothing left to be confiscated and that he could carry on preaching.

After a week in the country, Baxter's health greatly improved and so he took the opportunity to preach in some of the needy country churches in Hertfordshire and Buckinghamshire. Crowds of people, including many who had not been to a church for years, came to hear him. He sometimes preached to congregations of two to three thousand who listened to him with 'much attention and willingness'. The Quakers had a large following in Hertfordshire and, while in Rickmansworth, Baxter met their leader, William Penn,[1] in public debate. Baxter believed this was a very profitable exercise.

While Richard Baxter was away in the country the services in his meeting house were conducted by a Mr Seddon. During one service, while he was preaching, three J.P.s and several soldiers burst into the chapel in order to arrest Baxter. However, seeing their intended victim was not present, they changed the name on the warrant and arrested Mr Seddon instead! The poor man spent three months in jail before being released. Until now, most judges had been reluctant to enforce the harsh and unjust laws directed against the Nonconformists. However, in March 1676, the King commanded them to execute these laws with renewed vigour. As a leading Nonconformist, Baxter was especially targeted for their persecutions. Being denied the use of his own chapel (the former warrant against him still being in force), he preached at another chapel nearby. However, on 26 November 1676, six constables, four beadles[2] and several others were stationed at the chapel doors to arrest him. Baxter was able to elude them, but his life at this time continued to be a series of narrow escapes from the hands of his persecutors.

When Margaret Baxter died after a short period of illness on 14 June 1681, Richard felt her loss very deeply. 'Under the power of melting grief', immediately after her death he wrote, 'My dear wife did look for good in me, and more help in me than she found, especially lately in my weakness and decay. We are all like pictures that must not be looked at too near'. John Howe preached her funeral sermon as she was buried alongside her mother in Christ Church,[3] London on 17 June.

1. The founder of the colony Pennsylvania, U.S.A., which was named after him.
2. A beadle was an officer employed by a town or city council.
3. Christ Church in Newgate Street had been destroyed during the

'I am waiting to be next,' wrote Baxter, 'the door is open. Death will quickly draw the veil and make us see how near we were to God and one another, and did not sufficiently know it. Farewell vain world! And welcome true everlasting life'.

On Sunday, 14 August 1682, Richard Baxter was in great pain and weakness, and was only just able to preach twice. He thought he would never be able to preach again. However, he reflected that it was now twenty years since he had been ejected from the church on 'Black Bartholomew's Day', and during all that time, by God's mercy, he, and many others had been kept in relative 'peace' and freedom to serve the Lord, despite all the efforts of the Church and State to silence them. The Puritans never sought persecution, but neither did they flinch from suffering when they were called to endure it. 'It much more concerned us,' writes Baxter, 'to be sure that we deserved not suffering, than that we be delivered from it'.

Great Fire of London, although the churchyard had survived. It was rebuilt by the Second World War. No trace of this grave remains today. The church suffered bomb damage during World War II and only the steeple remains.

The heavenly hosts, world without end,
Shall be my company above;
And Thou, my best and surest Friend,
Who shall divide me from Thy love?

Richard Baxter

Chapter 9. 'Almost Well'

Late in 1682, at the age of sixty-seven, Richard Baxter was arrested once again. He had only just recovered from another bout of serious illness and was still extremely weak. He was charged with breaking the 'Five Mile Act' and was fined £190. On their way to the magistrates they were stopped by Baxter's doctor who immediately ordered him home to bed. The doctor then went to the magistrate and swore on oath that he would probably die if sent to prison. The magistrate consulted the King who told him to allow Baxter to die at home. However, they confiscated everything they could lay their hands on, even the bed he was lying on, in order to pay the fine. However, Baxter's friends bought most of his confiscated goods and 'lent' them back to him.

In February 1685, Charles II, the 'Merry Monarch', died after receiving the last rites and absolution from a Roman Catholic priest. He was succeeded by his brother, James II. He was a more ardent Catholic than Charles had been, and under his rule, the persecutions of Nonconformists continued with greater vigour than ever. In the same year, Baxter published a paraphrase of the New Testament. Because some of its passages seemed to be critical of the religious establishment, the authorities castigated it as being 'scandalous and seditious'. On 28 February 1685, Baxter was arrested and imprisoned yet again, this time under a warrant signed by the infamous Judge Jeffries.[1] He was released temporarily under a writ of *habeas corpus*[2] pending his forthcoming trial.

The trial took place in Westminster Hall in May that year. Baxter, now almost seventy years of age, and very feeble, pleaded 'not guilty' to the charges laid against him. Baxter's influential friends had secured for him four of the ablest barristers in the land, but it was obvious from the beginning of the trial that Jeffries had already decided what the verdict would be. When the defence requested more time to prepare their case, Jeffries raged, 'I will not give him a minute's time more to save his life'. During the trial, Jeffries seemed more like the prosecutor than the judge. Typical of his remarks about Baxter is: 'This is an old rogue, and hath poisoned the world with his Kidderminster doctrine ... he deserves to be whipped through the city'. Later, when Baxter was about to say something in his defence, Jeffries interrupted him. 'Richard, Richard', he roared, 'Dost thou think we'll hear thee poison the court? Richard, thou art an old fellow, an old knave; thou hast written books enough to load a cart, every one as full of sedition, I might say treason, as an egg is full of meat. Hadst

---

1. Chief Justice George Jeffries presided at the so-called 'Bloody Assizes' following an unsuccessful attempt by the Duke of Monmouth (one of Charles II's many illegitimate children) to overthrow James II. Jeffries was described as a man of shameless brutality who was often drunk and sometimes flew into a fury in court. He sentenced many hundreds to death on the flimsiest of evidence. In his cruelty, he often shamelessly mocked and jeered at those whom he had sentenced.

2. *Habeas Corpus* ('You must have the body') is a legal safeguard to prevent people being unlawfully imprisoned or restrained.

thou been whipped out of thy writing trade forty years ago, it had been happy. Thou pretendest to be a preacher of the gospel of Peace ... but ... I'll look after thee'. It was inevitable that the jury, carefully selected beforehand, would return their immediate and unanimous verdict of 'Guilty'. They did not even bother with the formality of retiring to consider the case. An appeal to the bishop of London proved futile.

When Richard Baxter returned to court in June for the sentence, he was fined 500 Marks[3] and ordered to remain in prison until he paid. Jeffries had wanted to have Baxter flogged through the streets of London, but his fellow justices would not allow so harsh a sentence. So, Baxter was imprisoned once more, in Southwark, for his faith, from June 1685 until November 1686. He received a steady stream of visitors during this time, including the young Matthew Henry, the famous commentator, who was then studying law in London. Because he was so old and feeble, Baxter's imprisonment attracted a great deal of sympathy from many people, and this became an embarrassment to the authorities. James II was also at this time seeking to win support from the Nonconformists. Therefore, when it became obvious that Baxter had no intention of paying the fine, Lord Powis interceded with the King and secured both his release and immunity from the 'Five Mile Act'.

In February 1687 Richard Baxter went to live in Charterhouse Yard in Clerkenwell where he assisted Matthew Sylvester's ministry as much as his health allowed. By December that year James II had lost almost all support so that he was forced to flee the country when William of Orange landed with his forces at Torbay. Thus ended the terrible tyranny of

---

3. A 'Mark' was a unit of currency based on the value of 8 ozs. of silver. In those days that was equivalent to 13s.4d.

the Stuart dynasty, and a Protestant succession to the throne was subsequently established by law. Baxter continued to write and to preach for as long as he could. After August 1691 he was no longer able to leave his house. However, every day, morning and evening, he would open his home to all who would join him in family worship. This he continued to do until illness confined him first to his room and finally to his bed. On Sunday 6 December 1691, Baxter was expecting to leave this world. Lifting up his eyes to heaven, he prayed, 'Lord, pity, pity, pity the ignorance of this poor city'. When his pain became very severe, he prayed to God for his release, but then checked himself: 'It is not fit for me to prescribe - when thou wilt, what thou wilt, how thou wilt'. The day before he died, he was visited by Dr. Bates and Mr Increase Mather (of New England). 'I have pain' he said, 'there is no arguing against sense, but I have peace, I have peace'. When asked how he was, he replied 'Almost well' meaning that he would soon be leaving his feeble body for an eternity of glory with Christ. During his last hours in this world, he found unspeakable comfort in thinking about some verses from Hebrews ch.12,

> *But ye are come unto mount Sion, and unto the city of the living God, the heavenly Jerusalem, and to the innumerable company of angels,*
>
> *To the general assembly and church of the firstborn, which are written in heaven, and to God, the Judge of all,*
>
> *And to the spirits of just men made perfect, and to Jesus the mediator of the new covenant* (Heb. 12: 22-24a, KJV).

This passage, he said, 'deserved a thousand thoughts'.

Richard Baxter summed up his life in these words, 'Weakness and pain helped me to study how to die; that set me on studying how to live; beginning with necessities, I proceeded by degrees, and now I am going to see that for which I have lived and studied'. Baxter had lived near to death for most of his life. His final words, spoken to his friend Matthew Sylvester, were, 'The Lord teach you to die'. Finally, at 4 a.m. on Tuesday 8 December 1691, in his seventy-sixth year, Baxter entered into his everlasting rest. He had 'fought the good fight, he had finished his course, he had kept the faith'. His earthly remains were laid to rest alongside those of his dear wife in Christ Church.[4] His funeral, according to Calamy, 'was attended by a most numerous company of all ranks and qualities, and especially of ministers, some of whom were Conformists, who thought fit to pay him that last office of respect'.

---

4.   See footnote 3, ch. 8.

GRACE
ESSENTIALS

LIVING WITH
THE LIVING GOD

GEORGE SMEATON
& JOHN OWEN

LIVING WITH THE LIVING GOD

George Smeaton & John Owen

Living with the Living God brings together two of the classic works on the person and work of the Holy Spirit from two of the most renowned theologians — George Smeaton and John Owen.

Part one looks at the Biblical teaching concerning the Holy Spirit, as Smeaton leads us on a journey of exploration through Scriptures teachings on the Holy Spirit.

Part two sees John Owen deal with the relationship between the believer and the Holy Spirit in our daily experience.

Living with the Living God provides an accessible and practical opportunity for the contemporary reader in understanding the work of the Holy Spirit.

George Smeaton and John Owen have written with characteristic depth on the person and work of the Holy Spirit. Their work, however, can feel somewhat daunting to the contemporary reader and so the treasure remains unearthed. This book resolves that difficulty. A really helpful doorway into the doctrine; it is lucid, accessible and surprisingly thorough for such a short volume. Readers will find it clarifies and edifies in equal measure.

Reuben Hunter,
Pastor, Trinity West Church, London

ISBN 978-1-78191-720-6

GRACE
ESSENTIALS

THE EXPERIENCE
THAT COUNTS

JONATHAN EDWARDS

The Experience That Counts

Jonathan Edwards

What does it mean to be a Christian? Is Christianity a matter of the intellect alone? What about desires, feelings and experiences? What is conversion? These questions are not new. Jonathan Edwards, the great American theologian tackled these, and many others, against the background of the First Great Awakening.

These questions and the answers Edwards gives to them are profoundly relevant to us today.

Find 'a guide for the perplexed' — a voice of clear biblical and spiritual sanity to lead us safely through the maze of contemporary confusion in this crucial area.

The spiritual value of Jonathan Edwards' Religious Affections can hardly be exaggerated. But the difficulty of the subject matter, combined with Edwards' tedious writing style and eighteenth century vocabulary, makes digesting it quite challenging for the modern reader. I am delighted that Christian Focus is releasing this modern edition of Edwards' classic work. Read this book. Let it read you. You will be challenged, convicted, and changed. I commend it highly.

Timothy K. Beougher,
Billy Graham Professor of Evangelism and Church Growth,
The Southern Baptist Theological Seminary, Louisville, Kentucky.

Edwards shows such humanity and realism as he tackles the issue of our emotional life. But he does so with great biblical clarity and charity, walking the tightrope between constraint and freedom. This is one of those books that every Christian should read more than once!

Mark Meynell,
European Director of Langham Preaching, London.

ISBN 978-1-78191-719-0

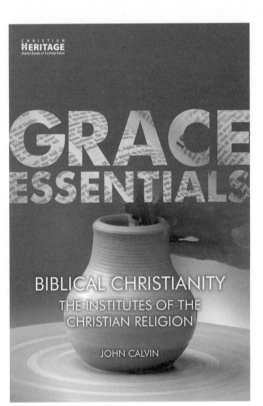

CHRISTIAN
HERITAGE
Useful Books of Lasting Value

GRACE
ESSENTIALS

BIBLICAL CHRISTIANITY
THE INSTITUTES OF THE
CHRISTIAN RELIGION

JOHN CALVIN

BIBLICAL CHRISTIANITY
THE INSTITUTES OF THE CHRISTIAN
RELIGION

John Calvin

Through exploring in turn the Father, the Son, and the Holy Spirit, Calvin's *Institutes* sought to achieve a 'knowledge of ourselves' in light of 'knowledge of God'. This work, foundational to theological thought for five centuries, is presented here in a faithfully edited version — perfect for enriching Bible Studies or devotionals.

John Calvin's Institutes of the Christian Religion stands like a majestic castle in the history of the Protestant Reformed tradition. Many Christians, intimidated by its size and scope, stand outside its gates, honoring it from a distance and wondering what lies inside. Here is an opportunity to wonder no more! This new edition of the reformer's magnum opus opens up the warmth and light of the Institutes to any reader. Scaled down in size and updated in language, this version serves up central aspects of Calvin's greatest work with such clarity that you will wonder why you waited so long to enter in. Read, feast and rejoice!

R. Carlton Wynne
Assistant Professor of Systematic Theology and Apologetics
Westminster Theological Seminary
Philadelphia, Pennsylvania

ISBN 978-1781-91965-1

Grace
Publications

Grace Publications Trust

Grace Publication Trust is a not-for-profit organisation that exists to glorify God by making the truth of God's Word (as declared in the Baptist Confessions of 1689 and 1966) clear and understandable, so that:

- Christians will be helped to preach Christ
- Christians will know Christ better and delight in Him more
- Christians will be equipped to live for Christ
- Seekers will come to know Christ

From its beginning in the late 1970s the Trust has published simplified and modernised versions of important Christian books written earlier, for example, by some of the Reformers and Puritans. These books have helped introduce the riches of the past to a new generation and have proved particularly useful in parts of Asia and Africa where English is widely spoken as a second language. These books are now appearing in editions co-published with Christian Focus as *Grace Essentials*.

More details of the Trust's work can be found on the web site at *www.gracepublications.co.uk.*

Christian Focus Publications

Our mission statement –

STAYING FAITHFUL

In dependence upon God we seek to impact the world through literature faithful to His infallible Word, the Bible. Our aim is to ensure that the Lord Jesus Christ is presented as the only hope to obtain forgiveness of sin, live a useful life and look forward to heaven with Him.

Our Books are published in four imprints:

CHRISTIAN
FOCUS

popular works including biographies, commentaries, basic doctrine and Christian living.

CHRISTIAN
HERITAGE

books representing some of the best material from the rich heritage of the church.

MENTOR

books written at a level suitable for Bible College and seminary students, pastors, and other serious readers. The imprint includes commentaries, doctrinal studies, examination of current issues and church history.

CF4•K

children's books for quality Bible teaching and for all age groups: Sunday school curriculum, puzzle and activity books; personal and family devotional titles, biographies and inspirational stories – because you are never too young to know Jesus!

Christian Focus Publications Ltd,
Geanies House, Fearn, Ross-shire,
IV20 1TW, Scotland, United Kingdom.
www.christianfocus.com